# SONOMA
## *Wine Tour*

A Vintage Image Book

PUBLISHED BY WINE APPRECIATION GUILD

The Wine Appreciation Guild is America's leading
publisher of wine books with over 60 titles in print.
Available in book stores and wine shops world-wide


Published by:
The Wine Appreciation Guild
360 Swift Ave.
S. San Francisco, CA 94080
(650) 866-3020 or (800) 231-9463
www.wineappreciation.com


Research Editor: Bryan Imelli
Design: Ronna Nelson
Author: Mildred Howie
Cartography: H. Hess, Global Graphics, Oceanside, CA


LIBRARY OF CONGRESS Catalog in Publication Data
Wine Tour
      "A Vintage Image Book"
      Previous publications classified separately and analyzed
      Content: [v.1] Sonoma Valley/Mildred Howie
      1. Wine and winemaking – California – Sonoma Valley – Collected works. 2. Sonoma Valley (Calif.)
      – Description and travel – Collected works. I. Mildred Howie.
TP557.W693 1984 917.94'10'0453          84-10390
ISBN 1-891267-09-4

PRINTED IN THE UNITED STATES OF AMERICA

# Table of Contents

# Sonoma County Wine Regions

 **W**elcome to Sonoma County's many wine regions. Unlike the Napa Valley, Sonoma County's wine-rich neighbor to the east, where scores of wineries are laid out in parallel rows along Highway 29 and the Silverado Trail, Sonoma County, with its million-plus acres, is more than twice as large and many times more complex. Physically its shape is rectangular, nearly as broad as it is long, encompassing within its boundaries a large part of the North Coast Ranges on its eastern side, and a long, rugged Pacific coastline on the west. Hilly ridges are separated by narrow, fertile valleys, and elevations range from sea level to 4,000 ft.

It was in these rich soils that the seeds of California's wine industry were planted, quite literally. People of two vastly different cultures did the planting. It is recorded that Russian settlers along the coast at what is now Fort Ross State Historical Park had planted vineyards as early as 1817. A few years later, in 1823, when the Franciscan Fathers established Mission San Francisco Solano in the Pueblo of Sonoma, they too planted vineyards, as was their custom.

With secularization of the Mission lands beginning in 1834, wine grapes got a solid boost with the appointment of General Mariano G. Vallejo as commandant of the Pueblo. Already a noted vineyardist, Vallejo increased his holdings, and was soon earning acclaim for his Lachryma Montes wines.

Sonoma was also the chosen home of the Hungarian Count Agoston Harazsthy, credited as the father of commercial wine production in California. Historical remainders of these players and dozens of other colorful characters in the drama of Sonoma County's attractions abound, affording a rich treasure to be explored by modern day visitors.

But wine isn't all that draws an appreciative audience to Sonoma County. Added to the lure of superb vintages, are the unmatchable wonders of rugged coastlines, statuesque redwoods, the serpentine curves of the Russian River, and dozens of reminders that Sonoma is today still an agricultural center with grazing dairy herds and gamboling sheep, orchards, row crops and several hundred farms open to a public seeking fresh fruit, vegetables, exotic plants or, in the season, Christmas trees.

Horticulturists flock to Sonoma County to visit the gardens and farm where naturalist Luther Burbank worked his wonders. Those of a literary bent home in on the Valley of the Moon where Jack London built, and lost his dream house. With 13 state parks and 33 regional parks and beaches those seeking active recreation, can find miles of hiking trails, limitless opportunities for boating, bike touring or horseback riding, or exercise their vocal cords, cheering for the home games of the Crushers baseball team.

Nor is there any lack of art, music, fairs and exhibitions, parades and fireworks displays. An abbreviated events calendar in this guide will identify some of the most outstanding. Needless to say, this brief overview cannot begin to encompass the kaleidoscope of activities that await in Sonoma County, nor can we list all of the hundreds of lodging availabilities or dining spots. What we have attempted to do, is select a wide diversity of what is available, and invite travelers to make their own additional discoveries.

Happy traveling!

# SONOMA COUNTY

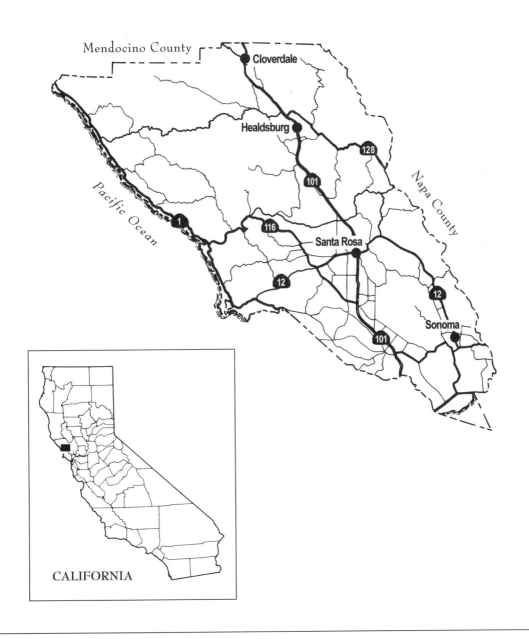

# Sonoma Valley

## Glen Ellen, Kenwood, Valley of the Moon and the Carneros Region

There are no real boundaries delineating the Valley of the Moon, but it is generally accepted that it lies on both sides of Highway 12, starting at the community of Oakmont on the north, and extending to the city of Sonoma on the south. There is more history crowded into this small stretch of land than in any other part of the vast county of Sonoma. In the city of Sonoma, the most populous community, the Franciscan Fathers erected Mission San Francisco de Solano, the final Mission in the chain of 21 that dotted El Camino Real from San Diego north. Portions of the original barracks once occupied by the soldiers of Col. Jonathan Stevenson's New York Regiment and the U.S. Army in the 1800s are now part of the state park system. Other historic homes and buildings are marked around the city with plaques and monuments. The most imposing memorial marks the spot in the Plaza, originally laid out by General Mariano Vallejo, on which the famous Bear Flag Revolt took place, and explains the "revolution."

On the southern edge of town is the original Buena Vista Winery, Sonoma County's premier commercial winery where the redoubtable "Count" Agoston Haraszthy planted his first successful vineyards, imported premium vines and shared his cuttings with growers throughout the state, earning for himself an identity as "the father of modern California viticulture."

A few short miles away from the bustling city of Sonoma is Glen Ellen, a quaint settlement nestled in a woodsy glen. Here the author Jack London lived and wrote from 1905 until his death in 1916. His novel, "Valley of the Moon," presenting a Utopian vision of a return to the land, was published in 1913. Now in the 48-acre Jack London State Historical Park, visitors can hike the trails the author trod, visit the ruins of London's ill-fated Wolf House, and browse through a collection of London memorabilia in "The House of Happy Walls," built by London's wife, Charmian as a memorial.

Wine buffs should not leave the area without visiting Benziger Family winery, on London Ranch Rd., to take the tram ride around the vineyards.

Four miles north of Glen Ellen, on Highway 12, is the small town of Kenwood, with a cluster of fine wineries, and a dedication to history with its carefully preserved Community Church and old stone railway depot. Kenwood is also the gateway to Sugarloaf Ridge State Park and Hood Mountain Regional Park, havens of scenic beauty for hikers, equestrians, and campers.

### THE CARNEROS

Even though, by the 1880s, the Carneros district was a flourishing grape-growing and winemaking area, half a century earlier, in the time of the Mexican land grants, it had largely been filled with herds of sheep, thus the name, "Carneros," meaning "ram." But even then, on the Napa side of Carneros, Jacob P. Leese, a son-in-law of General Mariano Vallejo, had planted a small vineyard on his Huichica Grant, and in the 1870s, an Indiana native, William H. Winter had constructed the first winery, Talcoa Vineyards, in the Carneros.

In 1983, the BATF granted the Los Carneros Appellation - the first U. S. appellation to carry its name into two counties - Napa and Sonoma. Of the two, the Sonoma section is the larger. Chardonnay and Pinot Noir are the primary grapes planted in the Carneros, accounting for approximately 85% of the planted acreage. Many visitors to the wine country, as they follow Highways 12/121 over the rolling hills striped with verdant vines are not even aware they are in the Carneros, although highway and grower signs are helping to keep the public better informed.

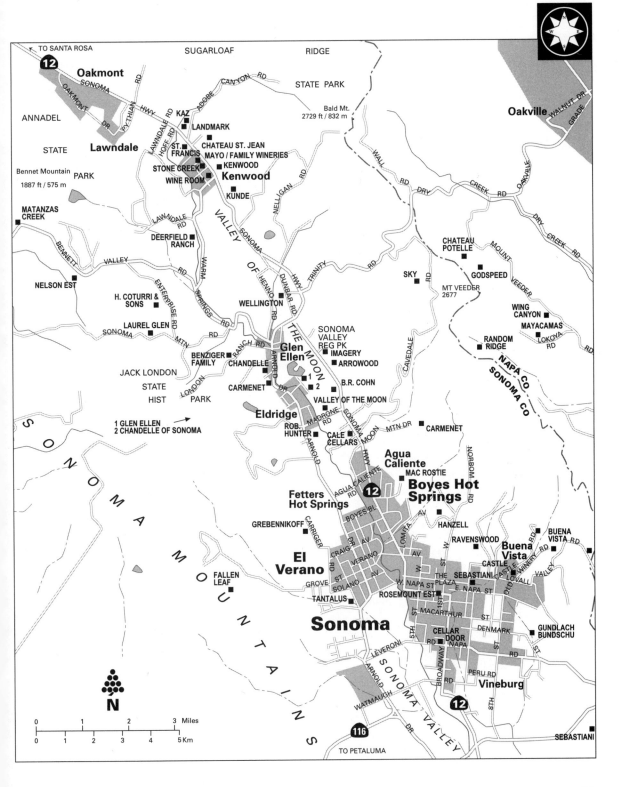

# Santa Rosa and Points South

When California ascended to statehood in 1850, General Mariano Vallejo was elected the first state senator for the Sonoma District. The seat of government, for the next three years was the city of Sonoma. Then, in 1854, by a bold legislative move, the rambunctious city of Santa Rosa lobbied a bill through the state legislature calling for the move of the county seat to Santa Rosa "the true center of Sonoma County." Following a wild two-day celebration, it is said, a band of Santa Rosans loaded the county archives into a wagon drawn by a mule team and, at break-neck speed, carried them away from Sonoma to Santa Rosa.

The origins of the city's name are obscure, particularly since it was a quite common name selected to honor St. Rose of Lima, the first female saint of the Americas. Many of the Spanish land grants included the name Santa Rosa, as well, from as early as 1833, and the Santa Rosa post office was established in 1852.

As the rail capital and merchandising center of the area, as well as being scenically beautiful Santa Rosa attracted hosts of new settlers. Some, like Thomas Lake Harris, who arrived in the late 1800s were more picturesque than others. Some, like Luther Burbank and, in more recent years cartoonist Charles Schulz, added greatly to the luster of the small town. The mystical prophet, Harris, and his Brotherhood of the New Life bought 1500 acres at Fountain Grove, which he called the Eden of the West. Here two of his followers, Missouri viticulturist, Dr. John W. Hyde and Japanese student, Kanaye Nagasawa, planted and tended vineyards which produced wines acknowledged as some of the best in the state both prior to and following Prohibition. Today the Fountain Grove label belongs to Martini & Prati winery, and a portion of the land is owned by the Byck family whose Paradise Ridge Winery above the still-standing round barn of the

Harris property produces elegant wines and preserves the heritage of Nagasawa.

Burbank, whose home and gardens in the heart of the city attract legions of visitors every year is credited with developing more than 250 fruits, and nearly as many decorative plants. Across Mendocino Avenue is Juilliard Park, a green oasis that is ideal for a planned or impromptu picnic. Other Santa Rosa Community parks include Howarth, offering hiking trails, tennis courts and a place to toss a ball around, and Spring Lake Regional Park, where visitors can swim, fish or hike.

For a glimpse of the past, there is the Sonoma County Museum and historic Railroad Square, and some excellent examples of Victorian architecture which have withstood earthquakes, fires and floods. The county fair is held at the Fairgrounds in Santa Rosa each July, and across the road is the Veterans Building, the venue for all manner of celebration and site of the Santa Rosa Farmers' Market. Luther Burbank Center, just north of the city, is home to the Santa Rosa Symphony Orchestra, and the setting for musical performances of every genre. Dramatic groups flourish and fine art galleries are dotted around the city. For more, see "Events."

## ROHNERT PARK

There are not a lot of grapevines in Rohnert Park, but this 39-year-old planned community is a good place to start exploring Sonoma County's wine country.

In its previous existence, Rohnert Park was a seed farm owned by the Rohnert family. When plans for development of the area were formulated in the late 1950s and early 1960s, provision was made for each "neighborhood" to be centered around a ten-acre school site, and have a park and proximity to a swimming pool and shopping center. Today there are ten parks and four pools within the city's boundaries. Also part of Rohnert Park are Sonoma State University (future home of the Maureen and Donald

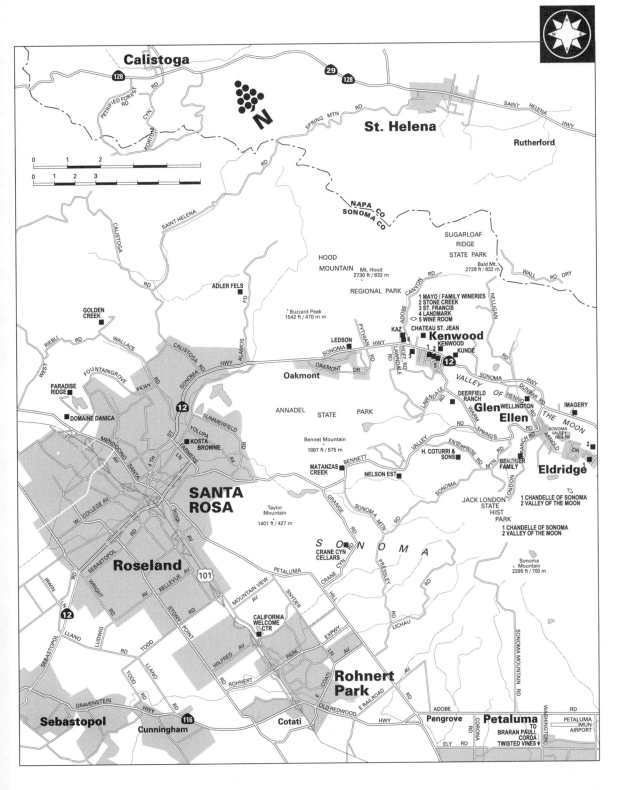

**Calistoga**

128

29 128

SAINT HELENA HWY

**St. Helena**

Rutherford

PETRIFIED FOREST RD

KORTUM CYN RD

SPRING MTN RD

N

NAPA CO
SONOMA CO

CALISTOGA RD

SAINT HELENA RD

SUGARLOAF RIDGE STATE PARK

Bald Mt. 2729 ft / 832 m

WALL RD DRY

HOOD MOUNTAIN

Mt. Hood 2730 ft / 832 m

REGIONAL PARK

NELLIGAN RD

ADLER FELS

GOLDEN CREEK

Buzzard Peak 1542 ft / 470 m m

ADOBE CANYON RD

1 MAYO / FAMILY WINERIES
2 STONE CREEK
3 ST. FRANCIS
4 LANDMARK
5 WINE ROOM

RIEBLI RD

WALLACE RD

WEST

FOUNTAINGROVE PKWY

LEDSON

PYTHIAN RD

SONOMA HWY

OAKMONT

KAZ

CHATEAU ST. JEAN

**Kenwood**

KENWOOD

Kunde

LAWNDALE RD

HOOF RD

1 2
3
5

12

PARADISE RIDGE

DOMAINE DANICA

12

SUMMERFIELD RD

YOLUPA AV

**Oakmont**

OAKMONT DR

ALAMOS RD

ANNADEL STATE PARK

DEERFIELD RANCH

WELLINGTON

**Glen Ellen**

VALLEY OF THE MOON

DUNBAR RD

HENNO RD

SONOMA HWY

IMAGERY

SONOMA VALLEY REG PK

ARNOLD

DR

2

1

**Eldridge**

MENDOCINO

SANTA

4TH

1ST

FARMERS LN

KOSTA BROWNE

Bennet Mountain 1887 ft / 575 m

BENNETT

MATANZAS CREEK

NELSON EST

H. COTURRI & SONS

WARM SPRINGS RD

ENTERPRISE RD

VALLEY RD

SONOMA MTN RD

BENZIGER FAMILY

LONDON RANCH RD

JACK LONDON STATE HIST PARK

1 CHANDELLE OF SONOMA
2 VALLEY OF THE MOON

1 CHANDELLE OF SONOMA
2 VALLEY OF THE MOON

**SANTA ROSA**

Taylor Mountain 1401 ft / 427 m

W COLLEGE AV

SEBASTOPOL RD

WRIGHT RD

**Roseland**

BELLEVUE AV

STONY POINT RD

101

GRANGE RD

CRANE CYN

CRANE CYN CELLARS

PETALUMA HILL RD

*S O N O M A*

SONOMA MTN RD

PRESSLEY RD

Sonoma Mountain 2295 ft / 700 m

IRWIN LN

12

LLANO RD

LUDWIG RD

SEBASTOPOL RD

TODD RD

LLANO RD

MOUNTAIN VIEW AV

SNYDER LN

CALIFORNIA WELCOME CTR

WILFRED AV

PARK AV

E COTATI AV

LICHAU RD

SONOMA MOUNTAIN RD

GRAVENSTEIN

**Sebastopol**

116

Cunningham

TODD RD

LLANO RD

ROHNERT

**Rohnert Park**

E RAILROAD AV

OLD REDWOOD HWY

Cotati

E COTATI AV

ADOBE RD

Pengrove

CORONA RD

ELY RD

**Petaluma**
TO
BRARAN PAULI, CORDA
TWISTED VINES ▼

WASHINGTON

RD

PETALUMA MUN AIRPORT

Green Music Center), the Dorothy Spreckels Performing Arts Center, the Community Sports Center and a pair of premium golf courses. It even has a home-town baseball team - The Sonoma County Crushers, part of the Western Baseball League.

## PENNGROVE AND COTATI

If the visitor to Sonoma County chooses to follow back-roads south from Rohnert Park to Petaluma, the route would pass along the eastern edge of Cotati and through the unincorporated hamlet of Penngrove, which looks very much as it did when it was settled at the turn of the century, with a pleasant gathering of houses, stores and barns. The old Penngrove Hotel, built to accommodate rail passengers passing through, still stands. Across Highway 101, west of Cotati, on Stony Point Road is another former hotel from the same era, Washoe House, now a popular restaurant.

All three municipalities lie within the four square leagues of the original Rancho Cotate land grant, presented to Captain Juan Castenada by General Mariano Vallejo in lieu of salary. After Captain Castenada sold the land, it passed through several ownerships until the greater portion of it was purchased, in 1849, by Dr. Thomas Stokes Page, and the site became known as Page's Station. One of the unique features of Page's Station, (now Cotati), is the hexagonal design in which the town is laid out. Each of the streets on the six sides was named for one of Dr. Page's brothers.

## PETALUMA

Although today it would be difficult to find very many chickens in the city of Petaluma, it was once known as the egg capital of the world thanks to Lyman Ryce, a settler from Canada who introduced white leghorn hens and his own invention, the incubator, into that part of the state in 1878. Petaluma, thanks to its 16-mile tidal estuary, Petaluma Creek, was already, at that time, a thriving shipping center for dairy products, eggs, potatoes, grains, fruit, livestock, wine and a host of other goods.

Decades earlier, General Mariano Vallejo had retained the Petaluma land grant for himself and on the east side of Petaluma Creek had dedicated his thousands of acres to raising sheep and cattle for the hide and tallow trade. For his family, he also constructed what is considered to be one of the most outstanding examples of Mexican hacienda architecture still standing. Though one wing is missing, Vallejo's massive Petaluma Adobe, has been authentically restored and has been designated a State Historical Park.

On the west side of the freeway, Petaluma has preserved its historic downtown with myriad examples of iron front buildings and Victorian splendor. A walking tour that leads past splendid century-old homes and gardens is a great way to spend a day, and even though the hens are gone, Petaluma still celebrates a gala Butter and Eggs Day with a colorful parade and street fair.

# Healdsburg

## Dry Creek Valley and Alexander Valley

Charming, quaint, and picturesque are all accurate words for describing the little city of Healdsburg, a dozen miles north of Sonoma's county seat in Santa Rosa. Healdsburg's present-day citizens and visitors have much to thank the town's founder Harmon Heald for. His greatest gift was his donation of the Plaza in the heart of town, dedicated as a "pleasure ground to be held free from business or public buildings forever." In recent years, there has been a glamorous refurbishing and restoration of the ancient buildings on the blocks surrounding the Plaza. One by one the handsome buildings with their gay awnings have attracted throngs of visitors to a dazzling array of fascinating boutiques. But all the attractions do not ring the Plaza. On the streets radiating out from this central point there are wine tasting rooms, 36 restaurants, a number of bakeries and a surprising collection of specialty shops. Healdsburg is a great walking town, with a numbered tree walk, and a tour of historic homes. A short walk from the Plaza is the world-recognized Sonoma County Wine Library, and in another direction, the Healdsburg Historical Museum, housed in an historic Carnegie library building. Bikes may be rented for exploring the back roads, and canoes are for rent at the city's Memorial Beach Park, and at Alexander Valley Campground.

Nestled, as it is, between and spreading into the fertile Dry Creek and Alexander Valleys, Healdsburg has always enjoyed a strong agricultural influence, and now counts as its neighbors almost 60 wineries and a dozen or more attractive bed and breakfast inns. Local farmers draw chefs and family cooks to their Farmers Market each Saturday morning and Tuesday evening, and many of the farms lie along the Sonoma County Farm Trails and may be visited during their peak seasons.

Alexander Valley is named for trapper-adventurer, Cyrus Alexander, who was deeded 9,000 acres of the fertile valley as pay for his services as manager of Captain Henry Fitch's Rancho Sotoyome. The Alexander family's cemetery and one of the original outbuildings have been preserved by the Wetzel family, which bought the ranch in 1963 from Alexander's heirs.

With the California wine renaissance, starting in the late 1960s, the Valley soon was filled with vines, primarily Chardonnay and Cabernet Sauvignon, and wineries sprang up on both sides of Highway 128 which leads the traveler through the luxuriant Valley from Cloverdale south.

On Healdsburg's western side is the Dry Creek Valley, with a road on either side of Dry Creek. Dry Creek Road leads past vineyards, wineries and farms to Lake Sonoma and Warm Springs Dam. Hikers, campers, boaters, fishers and lovers of the great outdoors find much to explore and enjoy, any season of the year. The road then climbs the hill and leads through slightly wild countryside to the Coast.

Traveling up West Dry Creek road, adventurers will find much to see, wines to taste and scenery to record photographically, or with paint and canvas, but no access to Lake Sonoma. There are, however, several bridges which cross between the two roads, so going or coming, new sights beckon.

The passing of the seasons in Healdsburg is saluted with parades, special events and concerts in the gazebo in the Plaza. (See Events).

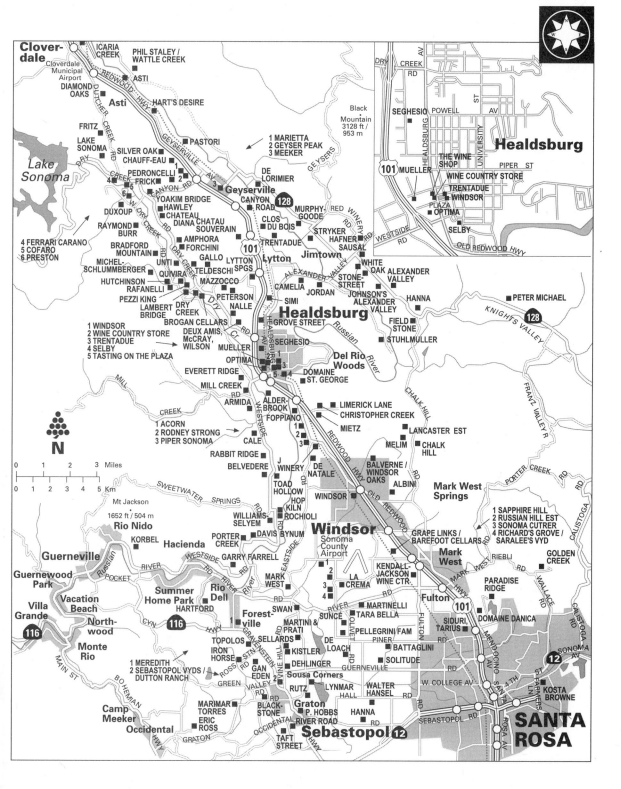

# Guerneville, Sebastopol, Russian River Valley

To the native Pomo Indian tribes, the Russian River was known as "Shabaikai" - the snake. The Russians, who established two communities on the Sonoma Coast in 1812, referred to the river as "Slavianka," - pretty Russian girl. Later Mexican settlers referred to it as El Rio Russo, giving it the name that finally stuck. The river's greatest influence has been on the lands referred to as the Russian River Valley, lying along the route of the river after it turns west just below Windsor.

The first significant agricultural crop in the area was potatoes, known as Bodega Reds. With the demand for paving stones as small villages grew into young cities, quarries were cut or blasted into the hillsides, but the greatest boom was in lumber. Mills sprang up along the river, and settlers poured in, creating new towns and changing the face of the landscape. One of these villages, at a great bend of the Russian River, took the name of lumberman George Guerne. Another, picturesquely situated in the rich eastern portion of the valley, became Sebastopol when a witness to a fight in Hibb's Saloon observed that the fight was "Hibb's Sebastopol" - a reference to a recent conflict in the Crimean War.

The arrival of the railroad in the 1870s brought the next major change. As branch lines extended towards the ocean more hamlets became towns, and villages became cities. Settlers with a strong agricultural heritage arrived, and new crops were planted along the banks of the river - apples, particularly in the Sebastopol locale, and grapes in great abundance. By the turn of the century, Sonoma County was the sixth most populous county in the state - even larger than Los Angeles. Thousands of those residents lived on or near the Russian River.

In the days when a horse and buggy was considered rapid transit, urbanites discovered the charm of the scenic area, and made pilgrimages to float down, fish in or picnic on the beaches up and down the river. Rail travel made the trip shorter and more comfortable, and to provide the visitors with accommodations and entertainment resorts began to spring up, and recreation became one of the main industries.

Though the dark years of Prohibition, many of the vineyards in the Russian River Valley survived and grapes were shipped to home winemakers across the country. With the rebirth of California's wine industry in the early '70s, men and women seeking a career change were drawn to this prime growing region and soon Highway 116 through Sebastopol and River Road along the banks of the river, were strung with long lines of flourishing grapevines and dotted with premium wineries. With time, the Russian River Valley gained renown for the Pinot Noir and Chardonnay wines its vines produce.

Small farms, growing specialty crops became more prominent, selling their wares at local Farmers' Markets and direct to the consumer traveling the Farm Trails. Chefs attracted by this bounty headed to the river region and opened scores of excellent restaurants, and today the Russian River Valley is saluted as a food and wine Mecca.

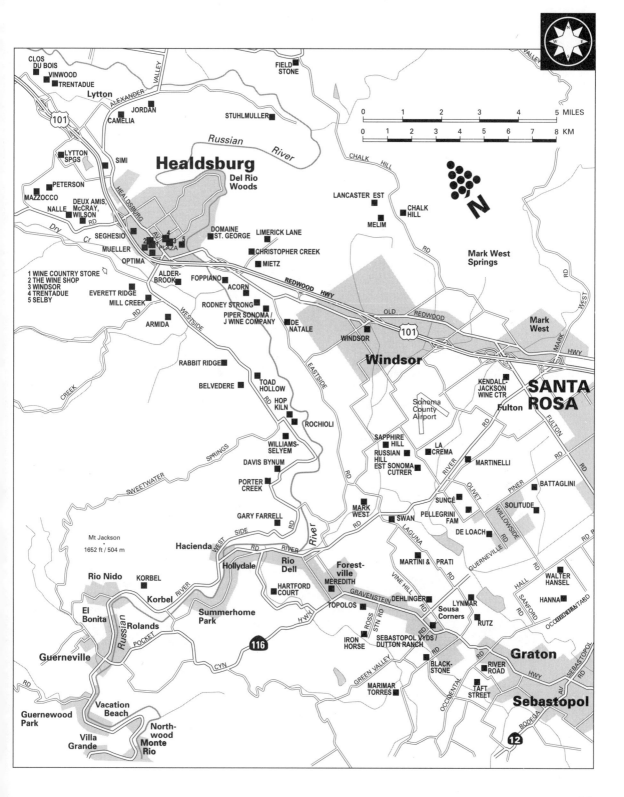

CLOS
DU BOIS
VINWOOD
TRENTADUE
Lytton
JORDAN
CAMELIA
STUHLMULLER
FIELD
STONE

Russian River

101

LYTTON
SPGS
SIMI
PETERSON
MAZZOCCO
NALLE
DEUX AMIS,
McCRAY,
WILSON
SEGHESIO
MUELLER
OPTIMA

**Healdsburg**

Del Rio
Woods

LANCASTER EST
CHALK
HILL
MELIM

Mark West
Springs

DOMAINE
ST. GEORGE
LIMERICK LANE
CHRISTOPHER CREEK
MIETZ

1 WINE COUNTRY STORE
2 THE WINE SHOP
3 WINDSOR
4 TRENTADUE
5 SELBY

ALDER-
BROOK
FOPPIANO
ACORN
EVERETT RIDGE
MILL CREEK
RODNEY STRONG
PIPER SONOMA /
J WINE COMPANY
DE
NATALE
ARMIDA

REDWOOD HWY

OLD REDWOOD

101

WINDSOR

**Windsor**

Mark
West

KENDALL-
JACKSON
WINE CTR

**SANTA
ROSA**

Fulton

RABBIT RIDGE
BELVEDERE
TOAD
HOLLOW
HOP
KILN
ROCHIOLI
WILLIAMS-
SELYEM
DAVIS BYNUM
PORTER
CREEK
GARY FARRELL

Sonoma
County
Airport

SAPPHIRE
HILL
RUSSIAN
HILL
EST SONOMA
CUTRER
LA
CREMA
MARTINELLI

BATTAGLINI
SOLITUDE

SUNCÉ
PELLEGRINI
FAM
DE LOACH

MARK
WEST
SWAN

Mt Jackson
1652 ft / 504 m
Hacienda

Rio Nido
KORBEL
Korbel

El
Bonita
Rolands
Guerneville

SWEETWATER

SPRINGS

WEST SIDE RD

RIVER RD

Hollydale
Rio
Dell
HARTFORD
COURT
Summerhome
Park

Russian

POCKET

Forest-
ville
MEREDITH

GRAVENSTEIN

TOPOLOS

116

IRON
HORSE

MARIMAR
TORRES

MARTINI & PRATI

DEHLINGER

SEBASTOPOL VYDS /
DUTTON RANCH

BLACK-
STONE
RIVER
ROAD
TAFT
STREET

LYNMAR
Sousa
Corners
RUTZ

WALTER
HANSEL
HANNA

**Graton**

**Sebastopol**

12

Vacation
Beach
Guernewood
Park
Villa
Grande
North-
wood
Monte
Rio

0    1    2    3    4    5 MILES
0  1  2  3  4  5  6  7  8 KM

N

It is safe to say that virtually any sort of food a visitor to Sonoma County might be in the mood to enjoy can be found within the county borders. While the entire state of California has attracted settlers by the millions, Sonoma County, because of its size, diversity of climate, and topography has enjoyed several migratory sweeps by people of a broad mix of ethnic cultures, who see many of the features of their homeland in the county.

Along with native dishes, introduced by each wave of new settlers, Sonoma County is blessed with a rich bounty of foods from the sea, herds of cows, sheep, and goats to provide milk and cheese, fields of vegetables both of old-fashioned varieties and exotic new introductions, berries of every hue, and orchards yielding sweet crops of apples, pears, peaches, apricots and meaty walnuts. Local chefs, many of whom have their own vegetable gardens right outside the kitchen door, are devoted shoppers at the direct-to-you Farmers' Markets and there is one in nearly every Sonoma County city.

These sources are part of the reason the county attracts so many creative and enthusiastic chefs. Just as it is nearly impossible to find a bad wine in Sonoma County, it is equally as unlikely that anyone would suffer through a really bad meal.

For those who prefer the familiar chain names, or are looking for something to eat on the run, all the familiar signs may be found along the highway. So, there is no reason to go hungry, and every reason to broaden your dining experience while a guest in the county.

As is true of our sections on wineries and lodging, it is impossible to give more than a broad picture of the variety, price range, and ambiance of all of Sonoma County's hundreds of restaurants, but we have tried to pick a representative sampling. We are sure you will find many to enjoy.

## AMIGOS GRILL & CANTINA
*Restaurant*

Every year since Amigos Grill & Cantina opened in 1997, manager Lori Gutierrez and Chef Rudy Gutierrez, owners of this delightful dining spot have been honored as having "The Best Family Restaurant in Sonoma" with additional awards for the "Best Mexican Food in Sonoma," and "The Best Margaritas in Sonoma." One visit will prove how accurate these awards are. Not only does Chef Rudy use the finest and freshest ingredients available when preparing his meals, but many of his recipes, from the Sonoran region of Mexico, have been handed down from generation to generation in his family. Rudy has been cooking since he was a young boy, and now with his own fine establishment he can show off his talents. The menu is extensive and fascinating with its mix of traditional Mexican fare and Rudy's own variations on familiar themes. For the health of his customers, Rudy uses only canola and soybean oil in his cooking. There are special menus designed for kids and for seniors, and the range of choices is generous, as are the servings.

*Amigos Grill & Cantina, 19315 Sonoma Hwy. (Highway 12), Sonoma, CA 95476. Telephone: 707-939-0743. Seating indoors and on patio. Full bar, featuring over 50 different kinds of tequila. Open seven days a week from 11:00AM - 9:00PM Reservations taken for parties of five or more.*

## APPLEWOOD INN & RESTAURANT
*Restaurant*

When Jim Caron and Darryl Notter, owners since 1985 of the former residence of the Santa Rosa Belden family in Pocket Canyon outside Guerneville, made the decision to add five suites to the Mediterranean style home, they also included a new restaurant. They constructed it in the style of a barn which had once stood on the property, designing a handsome beamed interior, twin fireplaces, and spacious viewing windows.

With the choice of Brian Gerritsen as executive chef, Jim and Darryl knew they were providing an unmatchable experience for the dining public. Gerritsen served as Chef de Cuisine at La Toque in the Napa Valley before being discovered by Jim and Darryl. The Applewood menu changes seasonally, and the specials are determined, in large part, by what is ripe and ready in the inn's orchard, vegetable and herb gardens. To complement the food choices, Applewood's prize-winning wine list offers more than 300 fine wines, most of them produced in Sonoma County. (See also, Lodging)

*Applewood Inn & Restaurant, 13555 Highway 116, Guerneville, CA 95446. Telephone: 707-869-9093, E-mail: stay@applewoodinn.com. Seats 60. Open for dinner Tuesday through Saturday. Price range $14.75 - $30.00 for entrees. Smoking only on smokers' balcony. No checks. Reservations advised.*

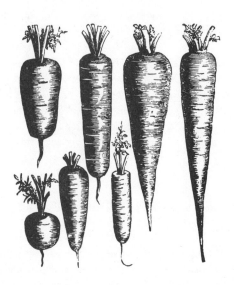

## ARRIGONI'S DELI CAFÉ
*Deli/Take Out*

Don't think of steam tables with trays of limp vegetables and unidentifiable meats when you are told that Arrigoni's is a cafeteria style gourmet deli. The emphasis is on gourmet, with a strong Italian influence. It's a pleasure to stand in line at the Arrigoni counter, surrounded by such an eclectic assembly of world cuisines. There are always seven or eight gourmet salads on the menu, two soups, one of which is always minestrone, and sandwiches made to the customer's choice right on the spot. The desserts are best described as "fabulous," and the espresso bar is always open. Established in 1937 on a busy corner in downtown Santa Rosa, Arrigoni's underwent a major face lift in 1980 but, knowing exactly what their customers liked, they left all the popular items on the menu and added a few more. A favorite spot for Santa Rosa's business community, Arrigoni's opens early, at 7:00 a m, with a breakfast menu that shows off all the standards, and spotlights its own exotic French toast with walnuts.

*Arrigoni's Café, 701 Fourth St., Santa Rosa, CA 95401. Telephone: 707-545-1297. Seats 70; patio seating for 20. Open 7:00AM - 4:30PM daily.*

## JOHN ASH & CO.
*Restaurant*

John Ash & Co. restaurant at Vintners Inn showcases the original wine country cuisine that made California dining famous. Chef Jeffrey Madura's inspired menu changes seasonally to take advantage of the abundance of locally grown fresh foods from the county's famous family farms. The ambiance at John Ash & Co. is unparalleled, with its stunning European architecture, stone fireplaces, and magnificent vineyard and garden views. An inviting, wisteria-covered terrace offers guests a relaxing outdoor milieu for Sunday brunch and weekday luncheons, where a surrounding view of 90 acres of lush green vineyards forms the perfect backdrop for a memorable meal. An outstanding wine cellar, recipient of the Wine Spectator's "Best of" Award of Excellence, boasts almost 600 labels, featuring the finest wines from Sonoma County's premier wineries and appellations, as well as many offerings from elsewhere in the United States and from around the world. Just two miles north of Santa Rosa John Ash & Co. offers the best of wine country cuisine for business gatherings, romantic dinners and vacation getaways. (See also Vintners Inn under Lodging)

*John Ash & Co.,4330 Barnes Rd., Santa Rosa, CA 95401. Telephone: 707-527-7687. Fax: 707-257-1202. Website: www.vintnersinn.com. Indoor and patio seating for 150. Open for lunch, Monday - Friday, 11:30AM; Dinner every day from 5:30PM, and Sunday Brunch. Reservations requested.*

## CAFE LA HAYE
*Restaurant*

If Frank La Haye, founder of the La Haye Metal Foundry, in 1936, could return to his building today, he would not only be dumbfounded by the changes, but delighted by the fine dinner he could enjoy at Cafe La Haye, while also enjoying the stimulating experience of browsing a show of the artworks by Brigitte McReynolds, and other local artists. Brigitte's husband, John McReynolds, co-owner, officiates as chef at the Cafe, demonstrating his talent for taking fine local ingredients, adding a nice touch of the cookery he learned while spending three years cooking in Europe, and transforming the blend into simple, yet sophisticated fare. The attractive setting and affordable prices make a visit to Cafe La Haye even more enjoyable.

*Cafe La Haye, 140 East Napa St., Sonoma, CA 95476. Telephone: 707-935-5994. E-mail: cafelahaye@vom.com. Website: www.cafelahaye.com. Serving dinner, Tuesday - Saturday, 5:30 - 9:00PM; Brunch, Sunday, 9:30AM - 2:00PM.*

## CAFÉ LOLO
*Restaurant/Catering*

When Chef Michael Quigley, co-proprietor of Cafe Lolo in Santa Rosa is asked to describe the restaurant he simply says, "Fun." Part of what makes it fun for Michael, and the Café's co-proprietor, his wife Lori (better known as Lolo) is that he can deal one-on-one with the farmers and the winemakers when putting together a menu. "And," he asks, "where else could I find such fresh and diverse quality in foods and wines? It is absolutely a chef's paradise." As a chef in this paradise Michael brings with him excellent training at Johnson & Wales University, and a wide range of experience gained working with the Sheraton Hotel chain, and smaller establishments. He and Lori opened their café in 1993. The bustling restaurant immediately received four star reviews, and continues to build a following of happily satisfied clientele with Michael's unique style of California Cuisine intertwined with a traditional Italian influence, served at the restaurant and through their catering services.

*Café Lolo, 620 Fifth St., Santa Rosa, CA 95404. Telephone: 707 576-7822. E-mail: cafelolo@sonic.net. Seating for 50 patrons. Private Room.*

## CHATEAU SOUVERAIN'S CAFÉ AT THE WINERY
Restaurant

"Being a chef at a winery restaurant is quite different from a regular restaurant," comments Martin Courtman, executive chef at the Café at the Winery. "If the restaurant chef doesn't have a chance to try his food in combination with just about every wine on the list, his pairing of flavors can be pretty hit or miss. Here I have the luxury of knowing what our winemaker, Ed Killian, was going for when he made the wines on our list, and consequently, I can highlight those flavors with whatever is fresh and in season."

Ask any Café diner, and they will assure you Martin

never misses the mark. Along with an inborn talent, Martin, a native of England, was schooled in classic French cooking techniques and thus believes that sauces are the key to effectively tying a dish to a particular wine. The bistro-style menu at Chateau Souverain suits Martin's love of cooking "from the market," using Sonoma County's vast resources, ranging from artisanal cheese, seafood, meats and free-range poultry, to organic produce. In order to maximize the freshness and reflect the season, Martin changes the menu regularly.

Arguably Chateau Souverain offers the most spectacular views in the county. Particularly awe-inspiring when viewed from the dining terrace.

*Chateau Souverain's Café at the Winery, 400 Souverain Rd., Geyserville, CA. Telephone: 707-433-3141, FAX: 707-857-4656. Website: www.chateausouverain.com. Seating 120 in dining room and 80 on the terrace. Serving lunch daily, 11:30AM to 2:30PM. Al Fresco, daily 2:30 - 5:00PM. Dinner, Friday, Saturday and Sunday, 5:30 to 8:30PM. Sunday Brunch, 11:00AM to 2.30PM.*

## COSTEAUX FRENCH BAKERY & CAFÉ
*Restaurant/Bakery/Take Out*
Seventy-five years ago an enterprising baker opened a small bakery shop in Healdsburg, on the main street, just a block or two north of the historic plaza. As the years progressed, other bakers took over the ovens, and in 1972 a French baker named Jean Costeaux put his name on the shop. In 1981 Karl Seppi, a former golf pro, and his wife, Nancy bought the establishment, and Costeaux carefully instructed the young couple in the art of breadmaking, with an emphasis on sourdough. When the bakery outgrew its original site, the Seppis built a new facility, adjacent to their first shop, and expanded their offerings, adding a unique outdoor cafe with a bistro menu. "We are what I guess you would call a 'full line' bakery," Nancy explains, "although most people probably don't know we make wedding cakes and specialty cakes like our triple chocolate mousse,

and we're the only place between here and North Beach in San Francisco where you can buy a fresh-baked St. Honore cake. The two most popular cookies are the chocolate crinkles and the blueberry sandwich, and we have been winning awards non-stop for our sourdough French bread." Specialties on the breakfast menu are Costeaux Quiche and a "build-your-own" omelet. Costeaux is also a great place to pick up a box lunch or arrange for a catered affair.

*Costeaux French Bakery & Café, 417 Healdsburg Ave., Healdsburg, CA 95448. Telephone: 707-433-1913, FAX 707-433-1955. E-mail: cfbake@aol.com. Seating, inside and on patio, 30. Open 6:00AM to 6:00PM, Tuesday through Sunday and until 10:00 PM Friday and Saturday serving French Onion Soup and Caesar Salad. Low to moderate prices.*

## CREEKSIDE BISTRO
*Restaurant*
Emile Waldteufel's charming Creekside Bistro provides friendly surroundings of hand-painted ivy on rustic walls, fresh flowers, and a view overlooking Santa Rosa Creek. Emile's skill in French Cuisine has attracted the notice of such publications as Gourmet Magazine and Vanity Fair. San Francisco Goodlife Magazine described Emile as a "perfectionist." Time Magazine praised his specialties. Chef Emile's great-grandfather, Pierre Gaston Domergue from Lyon, France, opened Domergue's Restaurant in Sausalito over 100 years ago serving discriminating diners who journeyed by ferry boat across the bay to dine at his establishment. Following in his ancestor's footsteps, young Emile earned his degree from San Francisco City College in their excellent hotel and restaurant program. He developed his skills working in some of the Bay Area's finest dining spots and spent a year in Bourgogne, France, at L'Hotel Maxime and La Palinurus. Back home, he opened Remillard's in Larkspur in 1989, before landing at the enchanting

bistro beside the Creek on Fourth St. Emile's dinners are praised as "an exercise in perfection," as he lends his fine touch to his exquisite sauces.

*Creekside Bistro, 2800 Fourth St., Santa Rosa, CA 95405. Telephone: 707-575-8839. Seats 48. Open for dinner only, 5:30PM -9:00PM, Wednesday - Sunday. Reservations recommended.*

## CUCINA RUSTICA - DEPOT HOTEL
### Restaurant

One of the things that makes the dining experience at Cucina Rustica in the beautifully restored Depot Hotel in the city of Sonoma so special is Chef/owner Michael Ghilarducci's deep appreciation of the variety and naturally healthy style of foods prepared by the home cooks in the small towns of Northern Italy, where he frequently visits. Raised in San Francisco's North Beach, where he worked in his father's kitchen from the age of 11, he went on to college and a formal culinary program, receiving formal training in the classical French tradition. To those experiences he has added his personal dedication to the preparation of all the meals served at Cucina Rustica, which he and his wife, Gia, purchased in 1985. All the basics are prepared from scratch - stocks, fresh soups, and sauces, and each course on the menu is prepared to order. All the items on the menu are available "to go." There is also a great deal of charm in the setting, with a colorful display of antique Italian china in the main dining room, and a quiet Italian garden with brick terraces, a reflection pool and fountain opening off the Garden Room.

*The Depot Hotel – Cucina Rustica, 241 First St. West, Sonoma, CA 95476. Telephone: Toll free: 800-200-2980 or 707-938-2980, FAX: 707-938-5103. E-mail: depothotel@worldnet.att.net. Website: www.depothotel.com. Seats 110 indoors, 90 in garden. Serves lunch, Wednesday – Friday, 11:30AM to 5:00PM. Dinner, Wednesday – Sunday, 5:00PM on. Reservations suggested.*

## CUCINA VIANSA
*Deli/Restaurant*

Where once the romantic young sipped sodas through a straw, searchers for the commonplace and rare in the way of Italian delicatessen items find all the scents and nuances of flavor of the Tuscan region of Italy at Cucina Viansa - a convenient, downtown miniature of the Italian Marketplace at Viansa Winery, just down the road. Like the winery, the deli is owned by Vicki and Sam Sebastiani whose love of good food and great cooking ingredients is legendary in the Sonoma Valley. Open seven days a week, Cucina Viansa offers take-out and table service, an ideal choice after a stroll around the Plaza.

*Cucina Viansa, 400 First St. East, Sonoma, CA 95476. Telephone: 707-935-5656, FAX: 707-935-5651. E-mail: tuscan@viansa.com. Website: www.cucinaviansa.com. Open Sunday – Thursday, 10:00AM- 7:00PM; Friday and Saturday, 10:00AM - 12:00AM. Last dinner seating 7:00PM.*

## DOWNTOWN BAKERY & CREAMERY
*Bakery/Ice Cream*

If you're a diner, demanding credentials before trying someplace new, check these out: Downtown Bakery & Creamery in Healdsburg was founded in 1987 by Lindsey Shere, Therese Shere, and Kathleen Stewart. Lindsey, a founding partner of Chez Panisse, Berkeley, is the author of Chez Panisse Desserts. Kathleen and Therese also were longtime employees at Chez Panisse before embarking on their own venture. With Kathleen now Downtown Bakery's remaining active partner, mouth-watering goodies include both basics and frills - from great breads to hot dog buns, wedding cakes and elaborate party desserts. For a faithful gathering of locals, the day can't start without the Bakery's sticky buns and cappuccino. Everything is made from scratch using local and organic products as much as possible. All ice creams are made from fresh eggs and cream. For home cooks Downtown Bakery provides ready-to-bake cookie dough, puff pastry and tart dough, short-cake mix and fruit crisp toppings.

*Downtown Bakery & Creamery, 308A Center St., Healdsburg, CA 95448. Telephone: 707-431-2719, FAX: 707-431-1579. Open Monday - Friday, 6:00AM - 5:30PM; Saturday, 7:00AM - 5:30PM, Sunday, 7:00AM - 4:00PM.*

## EQUUS RESTAURANT
*Restaurant*

There probably is no more dazzling wine display in Sonoma County than the Wall of Wine at Equus Restaurant at Fountaingrove Inn. Nearly 300 bottles of wine glow in the subdued lighting, so it is no wonder that the wine list at this outstanding restaurant, kept current and exciting by sommelier Larry Van Aalst, has won repeated awards for its diversity and content. For a pre-dinner glass of wine or a cocktail, the Equus Lounge is the friendliest spot in town, offering complimentary hors d'oeuvres each evening, Monday through Friday, from 4:30 - 6:30PM. Every Friday and Saturday night the bar offerings are enhanced by music played on the baby grand by a talented musician. Executive Chef Doug Lane displays his creative gift particularly well in his fine meats and seafood prepared on the wood-fired grill. There is a broad choice of lunch salads and sandwiches and an array of spectacular selections for an elegant dinner. (See also Lodging)

*Equus Restaurant, 101 Fountaingrove Parkway, Santa Rosa, CA, 95403. Telephone: 707-578-0149, FAX: 707-544-9374. E-mail: fgi@fountaingroveinn.com. Website: www.fountaingroveinn.com. Seating: 124 in main room, 50 in the lounge, 100 on the patio. Breakfast served 6:30AM to 10:30PM; lunch, 11:30AM to 2:00PM, dinner 5:30 to 9:30PM. Entrée prices $18.00 - $30.00. Reservations requested.*

## FITCH MOUNTAIN EDDIE'S
*Restaurant*

We are willing to bet that nowhere in Sonoma County can you enjoy that "day after Thanksgiving treat" of a turkey sandwich with dressing, potatoes, and gravy, any day of the year, except at Fitch Mountain Eddie's! And that's just one of the great items on the menu. Fitch Mountain Eddie's hamburgers are just the way you like them. In the cold winter months, there's always a pot of soup simmering on the back burner, and warm weather is celebrated with a firing up of the barbecue pit for ribs and barbecue chicken.

The original Eddie decided to join the California Highway Patrol, so Jim and Carol Mocci, pizza mavens from Pennsylvania, took over the rustic restaurant in 1994. With manager Kris Weaver on deck, visitors are greeted by a staff of happy, well-trained cooks and food servers who make Fitch Mountain Eddie's a welcoming spot.

*Fitch Mountain Eddie's, 1301 Healdsburg Ave., Healdsburg, CA 95448. Telephone: 707-433-7414. Indoor and patio seating. Open from 7:00AM to 9:00PM seven days a week.*

## GARY CHU'S
*Restaurant*

Dining at Gary Chu's shows that east and west can meet, and both benefit from the meeting. The cuisine blends traditional, contemporary and seasonal Chinese and Japanese cookery with the fine local ingredients so readily available in Sonoma County for a dining experience that shares the best of both worlds. To start the experience, begin with Gary Chu's signature Rainbow, Caterpillar and Dragon Maki sushi rolls, and continue with an entrée of Chicken with Fresh Mango, or Seafood Battayaki. The well selected wine list features a wide range of premium Sonoma County wines, imported beers and exotic premium sake. Grace notes are the large freestanding aquarium at the entry, and the Asian-influence art displayed throughout the dining area. Gary Chu's features executive style seating, and for those important private parties, there are nicely appointed private dining rooms.

*Gary Chu's, 611 Fifth St., Santa Rosa, CA 95401. Telephone: 707-526-5840, FAX: 707-526-3102. Open Tuesday through Sunday from 11:30AM, serving lunch and dinner. Entrée prices range from $7.95 - $24.00.*

## THE GIRL & THE FIG
*Restaurant*

Long a dining destination in the hamlet of Glen Ellen, on December 1, 2000, The Girl & The Fig moved into the historic Sonoma Hotel just off the Plaza in Sonoma. All that has changed is the location. The staff, the slogan - "country food with a French passion" - and the menu remain the same, only sparked up with some delicious specials. Also in place, but even more delightful is the Rhone Only wine list offering diners an array of seldom seen and truly enjoyable varieties whose original home was in France's Rhone region. Particularly enjoyable are the flights offered: tasting size samples of three of the same varietal as presented by three different producers, or three to five different varietals, which gives the diner a chance to compare and contrast the nuances between the wines and how they interact with the stunning menu choices.

*The Girl & The Fig, 110 West Spain St., Sonoma, CA 95476. Telephone: 707-938-3634, FAX: 707-938-2064. Website: www.thegirlandthefig.com. Seating: 75 in the main room, 50 in the patio. Entrees $18.00 - $21.00. Reservations requested.*

## HEALDSBURG CHARCUTERIE
*Restaurant*

"When I was a small boy," says Patrick Martin, owner, with his wife Robin, of The Healdsburg Charcuterie, "the family was having dinner in a restaurant to cele-

brate my grandfather's birthday, and, at that moment, I knew that what I wanted more than anything else was to be a cook and have my own restaurant." His route to that goal began at the Cuisiners de France, when he was 14. He served his apprenticeship at Roux Bros. in London, then headed for the United States, where he worked his way across the country in a number of highly popular restaurants, including Square One and Masa's. When the young couple moved to Healdsburg their timing was perfect. They met the owners of the Charcuterie who had just decided to sell the restaurant, and in June, 1995 Patrick and Robin became sole owners of the small, attractive restaurant just across from the historic plaza. Patrick describes his cuisine as French Mediterranean, with California fresh produce, meats, poultry and seafood - most of it grown within a 25-mile radius of the restaurant. With 67 wineries no farther than a 20-minute drive away, the wine list is extensive and filled with the premium offerings of his neighbors and customers.

*Healdsburg Charcuterie, 335 Healdsburg Ave., Healdsburg, CA 95448. Telephone: 707-431-7213, FAX: 707-431-0429. E-mail: charcuterie@cs.com. Website: www.charcuterierestaurant.com. Table seating - 33; three seats at counter. Serves breakfast, Monday through Friday, 7:00 - 10:30AM; lunch, 11:30AM to 3:00PM, Monday through Friday; Saturday noon - 3:30PM. Dinner hours: Sunday - Thursday, 5:00 - 9:00PM. Friday and Saturday, 5:30 - 9:30PM. Prices in moderate range. Lunch reservations for parties of five or more.*

## JELLYFISH
*Restaurant*

Jellyfish Restaurant at the Sheraton Petaluma Hotel features the inspired menus of executive chef Barbara Hom, one of Northern California's favorite chefs for 18 years. At Jellyfish Barbara's talents and creativity offer guests an uncommonly exquisite dining experience with an explosive fusion of flavors combining cuisine from

Asia and the Mediterranean. Prior to dining, guests may wish to try one of Jellyfish's specialty cocktails, a cup of sake or a glass of wine from a list of 30 choices by-the-glass. To go with dinner, there is a global six-page wine list that presents a number of half bottles, ideal for a couple to share. A relaxing view of the boats in the marina and the high river bridge is pretty as a picture through floor to ceiling windows. With an elegant lounge, full service cocktail bar, patio dining and raw bar, Jellyfish is perfect for any formal or informal occasion.

*Jellyfish at the Sheraton Petaluma Hotel, 745 Baywood Drive, Petaluma, CA 94954. Telephone: 707-283-2900. Jellyfish seats 65 inside and is open daily for breakfast, 6:30AM - 11:00AM; lunch from 11:30AM - 2:30PM, and dinner from 5:30PM - 10:30PM. Reservations are suggested for lunch and dinner.*

## JIMTOWN STORE
*Picnic Provender On-Site or To Go.*

Until the late John Werner and his wife, Carrie Brown chanced upon Jimtown Store, in the heart of Alexander Valley, the old-fashioned country-store had been locked and gathering dust for six years. A landmark in the area once known as Jimtown, Jimtown Store was established in 1893 and served as a post office and a source for such basics as flour, sugar and farm tools. Taken over by the Goodyear family at the turn of the century, it served as the place to go for anything you needed, from sewing thread to fishing tackle. Carrie and John, both from New York, though widely traveled citizens of the world, transformed the tiny store into an all-American country store with worldly sophistication and an emphasis on food. Now an important part of the wine country life, Jimtown Store supplies old-fashioned box lunches, special picnics and carry-away, and a line of Jimtown's own spreads, sauces and dips.

*Jimtown Store, 6706 Highway 128, Healdsburg, CA 95448. Telephone: 707-433-1212, FAX: 707-433-1252. E-mail: jimtown@jimtown.com. Website: www.jimtown.com. Seating inside, one small table and counter top, picnic tables on patio seat 26. Open weekdays from 7:00AM - 5:00PM, weekends, 7:30AM - 5:00PM.*

## JOSEF'S RESTAURANT AND BAR
*Restaurant/Catering/Take Out*

Chef Joseph Keller's fans, who have enjoyed and praised his culinary talents for more than 20 years in Sonoma County also enjoy a singular extra - Josef's Newsletter "Shortie." Short it may be, but in it Josef finds room to wax poetic about the change of seasons in Sonoma County, give a quick report on his trip to his homeland in Switzerland, and share an exclusive recipe. The "Shortie" also contains a lot of news about special holiday brunches and dinners, and announcements of new features such as the three course prix fixe Early Bird Special (Tuesday through Friday, 5:00 - 6:00PM) and Happy Hour (Tuesday through Friday, 4:00 - 6:00PM) with Josef's own selection of complimentary hors d'oeuvres. For lunch at Josef's, the emphasis is on light and hearty meals to enjoy at your leisure or to fit into a busy schedule. Lunch and dinner menus change every two weeks at Josef's, set like a jewel in the historic Hotel La Rose in Railroad Square.

*Josef's Restaurant and Bar, Hotel La Rose, 308 Wilson St., Santa Rosa, CA 95401. Telephone: 707-571-8664, FAX: 707-571-8760. Lunch is served from 11:30AM - 2:00PM, Tuesday through Friday, and dinner is served every evening, starting at 5:30PM. Banquet rooms for parties of 12 - 200 are available. Josef's offers catering services, and take out when ordered in advance. Entrée prices range from $15.50 - $21.50.*

## KENWOOD RESTAURANT & BAR
*Restaurant*

Maybe everybody doesn't know your name at Kenwood Restaurant, but Max and Susan Schacher, owners since 1986, have the knack of making their guests feel completely at home, well-fed and welcome. They call their cuisine Modern Continental and reading down the menu the delighted diner will indeed find tempting versions of Italian risotto, middle eastern dolmas, French escargots and, one of the favorites with local dinners, from our own continent, Dungeness Crab Cakes. The menu is decidedly thoughtful, with a fine list of small courses, as well as the larger main course portions. Most of the vegetables and herbs come from the Schachers' own gardens, and making the most of that freshness is Chef John Pardy's specialty. The patio is a favored spot for enjoying lunch or dinner in a scenic vineyard setting, and on nippy evenings, a spot beside the fireplace in the bar is irresistible.

*Kenwood Restaurant & Bar, 9900 Highway 12, Kenwood, CA 95452. Telephone: 707-833-6326, FAX: 707-833-2238. E-mail: KRB833@aol.com. Seating, 60 in main room, 35 on patio. Continuous service, 11:30AM to 9:00PM, Wednesday through Sunday. Prices for entrees $12.00 - $27.00. Reservations requested.*

## KIRIN RESTAURANT
*Restaurant/Take Out*

The restaurant takes its name from Kirin, a legendary Chinese creature, originally reputed to appear whenever a Chinese saint was born. Today Kirin is worshipped as a harbinger of happy and festive events. One step through the door of the colorful restaurant is positive proof that Kirin has shed his gracious blessing on all who enter. Noted for their Peking cuisine, Kirin also offers a full menu selection of Mandarin and Szechuan dishes for

lunch, dinner and take out. Whichever style of cooking appeals to the diner, each dish is a glorious mixing and blending of colors, aroma, flavors and textures.

*Kirin Restaurant, 2700 Yulupa Ave., #3, Santa Rosa, CA 95405. Telephone: 707-525-1957, FAX: 707-525-1959. Website: www.kirin-restaurant.com. Seating for 80, with four patio tables. Open for lunch Monday - Saturday, 11:30AM - 2:30PM. Dinner service, Sunday - Thursday, 4:30PM - 9:30PM, Friday 4:30PM - 10:00PM, Saturday 2:30PM - 10:00PM.*

## LaSALETTE RESTAURANT
*Restaurant*

To fully enjoy the Portuguese cuisine and the cultural experience of dining at LaSalette Restaurant, it is essential to understand the historical background of Portugal, her former colonies and their foods. Each element in the dining experience has purpose and significance. Every meal tells a story. Historically, Portugal and her colonies were responsible for importing and exporting many ingredients which have defined cuisines across the globe, including spices, tomatoes, chocolate and peppers. Chef/Owner Manuel Azevedo grew up in the Azores, spending time in the garden planting and harvesting the vegetables his mother used in her cooking. In the kitchen, he was led by his mother's inspiration. Finally, with great bravery, young Azevedo immigrated to northern California, and, to the joy of those who like adventure with their food, opened LaSalette, named after his mother. His dishes might best be described as modern adaptations of old world peasant food, served in a formal, yet relaxed atmosphere.

*LaSalette Restaurant, 18625 Sonoma Hwy. 12, Sonoma, CA 95476. Telephone:707-938-1927. Website: www.lasalette-restaurant.com. Open hours: Wednesday - Saturday, 5:00 - 9:00PM, Sunday, 2:00 - 9:00PM. Seating, 40 inside, 25 on patio.*

## MANZANITA RESTAURANT
*Restaurant*

One of the newest of Healdsburg's growing collection of fine and unique restaurants, Manzanita is the culinary child of Carole and Mike Hale, former creator and owners of Willowside Café. After discovering a handsome hundred-year-old building just a block from the historic Plaza, Carole and Mike embarked on a complete remodel to create a warm, rustic, comfortable environment in which to enjoy their Mediterranean-based foods, and comprehensive wine list - heavy on local wines, but including examples of some of the best vintages from around the world. Both the executive chef, Bruce Frieseke and sous chef, Moishe Hahn-Schuman worked with Carole and Mike at Willowside, which assures fans of the former restaurant that quality and versatility of the menu is still set to a remarkably high standard. Be sure to check the dessert menu before you order, so you'll be sure to have room for such delicacies as the Meyer Lemon Pot de Creme, or Chocolate-Hazelnut Tartlet.

*Manzanita Restaurant, 336 Healdsburg Avenue, Healdsburg, CA 95448. Phone and FAX: 707-433-8111. Seating in main dining room, 48, in bar dining room, 20 with six stools. Private Wine Cellar seats eight. A la carte entrees, $16.00-$24.00. Reservations suggested.*

## MIXX RESTAURANT
*Restaurant*

Mixx Restaurant opened in May, 1989 in the building that was once occupied by the historic Silver Dollar Saloon. The magnificent hand-carved bar was built in Italy in the late 1800s and shipped around the horn to San Francisco, arriving at the saloon in 1904. There is a nostalgic hint of the past in the gleaming table settings, reflecting back the soft light from the exquisite trumpet blossom chandeliers. But the high style of formal dining is tempered by the warm personal welcome of chef/owners Kathleen and Dan Berman and their gracious and well-informed staff.. Both Kathleen and Dan are graduates of the California Culinary Academy and both have been showered with distinguished awards for the restaurant, for Kathleen's desserts, and for Dan's superb wine list. Dan's emphasis in his cuisine is on local produce and products, so the menu changes seasonally and always shows a delightful freshness of flavor. Many items are "heart-friendly," and the chef is happy to customize regular menu items for those who prefer a vegetarian diet.

*Mixx Restaurant, 135 Fourth St., Santa Rosa, CA 95401. Telephone, 707-573-1344, FAX:707-573\0631. E-mail: mixx@ap.net, Website: www.mixxrestaurant.com. Seating: 110. Lunch is served Monday - Saturday from 11:30AM - 2:00PM. Dinner is served Monday through Saturday, starting at 5:30PM. Reservations are advised.*

## NIGHT OWL CATERING
*Catering*

Over the past 18 years, Night Owl Catering, an award-winning, full service catering company, has established a reputation for innovative menus, high quality cuisine and flair in presentation. Chef de Cuisine Catherine Plav-Driggers has an exotic background as executive chef and chef-owner of restaurants in California, England and the Caribbean. With these influences to draw on Night Owl Catering is known for what is called "global eclectic." With an emphasis on the use of seasonal local ingredients and a fully customized approach to each event, Night Owl Catering also places strong emphasis on wine pairing, for corporate meetings and receptions, weddings and wine country events with ten or more in attendance.

*Night Owl Catering/Barbara Hom, 821 Russell Ave., Suite L, Santa Rosa, CA 95403. Telephone: 707-579-7801. FAX: 707-579-7803. E-mail: nightowl2@earthlink.net. Website: www.nightowlcatering.com.*

## OSAKE
*Restaurant*
The tone of the tranquil dining experience you are going to enjoy is set as you walk through the entryway at Osake, where a large, freestanding aquarium, filled with the flitting shapes of jewel-tone fish captures the visitor's eye and fancy. Around the dining room, the graceful art forms of the Orient continue to entrance the guest, and then the menu and wine list arrive, and it is time to satisfy the senses that sort out the exciting aromas and flavors of a perfectly prepared meal. As an appetizer the choices are many - some traditional and expected, others, like the Japanese Carpaccio, unusual and unexpected. With the dinner the beverage choice covers an excellent selection of Sonoma County premium wines, unique imported beers and exotic sakes.

*Osake, 2446 Patio Ct., Santa Rosa, CA 95401. Telephone: 707-542-8282, FAX: 707- 579-4880. Osake is open Monday through Thursday, 11:30AM - 9:30PM, Friday, 11:30AM - 10:0PM, Saturday, 4:30 - 10:0PM. Entre prices range from $7.95 - $24.00*

## RUSSIAN RIVER VINEYARDS RESTAURANT
*Restaurant*
Even if the food were not the superb blend of Greek, Mediterranean, and California cuisine that it is, the restaurant at Topolos Russian River Vineyards would be an exciting destination. The three separate dining rooms in the century old farmhouse set above the winery's tasting room, offer impeccable service and country home comfort, but what is even more appealing, particularly in the summer months, is the shady fountain-patio with its koi pond, surrounded by native Sonoma County riparian plants. Always a delicious specialty on the menu is lamb - as a keftede lamb patty in pita for lunch, or en brochette, ground in eggplant moussaka, or as a generous eight-bone rack of lamb in port sauce for dinner. Roast duckling and pork tenderloin are also menu favorites, and to make even this fine food taste

better, there is the Vintner's Experience, four pours of wine chosen to complement each course of the meal.

*Russian River Vineyards Restaurant, 5700 Gravenstein Hwy., North, Forestville, CA 95436. Telephone reservations: 707-887-1562, FAX: 707-887-1399. Website: www.topolos.com. Seating capacity, inside – 90, outside – 120. Groups of up to 200 can be accommodated in a reception setting. Open seven days a week, during summer and early fall. Closed Mondays and Tuesday off-season. Lunch is served 11:30AM – 2:30PM; dinner beginning at 5:30 and Sunday Brunch 10:30AM – 2:30PM.*

## SADDLES RESTAURANT
### Restaurant

There's a promise a steak lover just can't ignore on the menu at Saddles. It says: We specialize in serving the finest midwestern corn-fed USDA Prime beef. And for those who aren't sure what "Prime" is, Saddles explains that only 2% of all beef qualifies for the USDA Prime grading that is, in a manner of speaking, assuring the diner that the meat is more tender, juicy and full of flavor. Of course, it doesn't have to be beef to be a super, delightful meal at Saddles. Executive Chef Dana Jaffe puts her own individual touch on the finest freshest seafood, al dente pasta and grilled chicken. One piece de resistance is the platter of barbecued baby back ribs with steak fries! Prime Rib is on the cart Sunday and Wednesday evenings; pot roast, Monday and Tuesday, and petite filet with lobster tail each Friday and Saturday. Saddles is set in an historic barn at MacArthur Place, an inn and spa located on the former Burris-Good estate, and this inimitable setting is available for conferences and private parties. (See also Lodging).

*Saddles Restaurant, 29 E. MacArthur St., Sonoma, CA 95476. Telephone: 707-933-3191, FAX: 707-933-9833. E-mail: info@macarthurplace.com. Website: www.macarthurplace.com. Hours for lunch are 11:30AM–*

*2:30PM to 5:30 PM Friday-Saturday; dinner 6:30 – 9:30PM, daily. Seating inside: 65, patio 40, bar 18. Entrée prices range from $13.95 – $36.95. Gift certificates available in lobby of MacArthur Place hotel, adjacent.*

## SANDPIPER
### Restaurant

There's a wonderful, "come as you are, everybody's welcome" feel to the Sandpiper, set beside the water at Bodega Bay. It's a homey spot, favored by the locals, and treasured by the traveler with a craving for fine seafood. At the top of the list of favorites is the Sandpiper's clam-rich clam chowder. Chefs Yves Larguinat and Mike Hedden are also celebrated for crab cioppino, seafood specials, the best fish and chips in town, and nothing is more satisfying for the sweet tooth than the Sandpiper's homemade bread pudding with a to-die-for caramel sauce. Whenever the hunger pangs strike, you can head for the Sandpiper, open every day from seven AM, serving breakfast, lunch and dinner. Magnificent as the view is from the dining room, it still takes second place to the phenomenal food at Sandpiper.

Snyder, while the all-American Wine List is personally selected by Laura Kudla.

In addition to regular service, Sassafras offers an ongoing program of special food & wine events, and is available for private parties, banquets, and off-premise catered events.

*Sassafras Restaurant & Wine Bar, 1229 No., Dutton Ave., Santa Rosa, CA 95401. Telephone: 707-578-7600. FAX: 707-578-7888. E-mail: sassafras@sonic.net. Seating: inside, 100 – patio, 60 – bar, 25. Lunch served Monday through Friday from 11:30AM to 2:00PM. Dinners nightly 5:30PM to 9:00PM.*

## SEA RANCH LODGE
*Restaurant*
After being seated and receiving your menu, it can take some extra time to get around to ordering so spectacular and ever-changing is the panoramic view from the Restaurant at the Lodge and the light-filled solarium. Just watching the meadow grasses bow in the wind is eye-catching. Add to that simple view the possible sighting of a pod of cavorting whales, kites soaring above the bluffs and a virtual parade of shore and sea birds and it is a sure bet you're in for an extended lunch hour. Evening sights, though more subdued bring the added element of stars and constellations shimmering above the restless Pacific. Then, there is the food. Executive Chef Jeffrey Longenecker blends his Coastal Cuisine with a beautiful simplicity of presentation that fits well into the rusticity of the Lodge and the natural beauty beyond the windows. Don't be surprised to see him emerge from the kitchen to chat about his favorite dishes and how he came to create them. For a longer visit with Jeff, check the schedule of Winemaker Dinners presented at the Lodge each month or stop by for Chef Longenecker's fabulous Sunday Brunch. When making dining plans for the Restaurant at the Lodge, breakfast, lunch or dinner, it is best to call ahead for reservations. (See also Lodging).

*Sandpiper Restaurant, 1410 Bay Flat Rd., Bodega, CA 94923. Telephone: 707-875-2278. Website: www.sandpiperrestaurant.net. Seats 50. Open daily, 7:00AM- 9:00PM.*

## SASSAFRAS RESTAURANT & WINE BAR
*Restaurant*
Located in the Santa Rosa Business Park, Sassafras is open for lunch and dinner and features a Wine Bar offering a great selection of wines for tasting as well as a complete complement of premium spirits.

Both the menu and wine list draw exclusively from the produce of North America. The menu, featuring regional specialties from all over the US. Canada, Cuba, the Caribbean, etc., showcases the talents of Chef Scott

*The Sea Ranch Restaurant at the Lodge, 60 Sea Walk Dr., The Sea Ranch, CA 95497. Telephone: 707-785-2371. Reservations, toll-free 800-732-7262. Website: www.searanchlodge.com. Serves breakfast, lunch, dinner and Sunday Brunch. Special light food service in the bar. Seating for 75.*

## SONOMA-MERITAGE RESTAURANT & OYSTER BAR
*Restaurant*

Chef Carlo Cavallo was working as a research associate in genetic engineering at the University of California Medical Center in Los Angeles when a friend convinced him he should become a chef. It didn't take much convincing — Carlo was already catering lavish dinner parties for the doctors and administrators of the hospital to earn extra money. After establishing a dedicated fan base as the Executive Chef for Giorgio Armani's Restaurant in Beverly Hills, he opened Sonoma-Meritage Restaurant & Oyster Bar. "I opened Meritage in the heart of Sonoma Country expressly to take advantage of the year-round abundance of locally grown fresh products, artisan food producers and superior wines." For Cavallo, Meritage offers the perfect venue to blend the tasty victuals of his European heritage with California's wine country sophistication.

*Sonoma-Meritage Restaurant & Oyster Bar, 522 Broadway, Sonoma, CA 95476. Telephone: 707-938-9430, FAX: 707-938-9252. Website: www.sonomameritage.com. Seating: 175. Open Wednesday-Sunday, 8:00AM - 9:00PM; Monday, 11:30AM - 9:00PM; closed Tuesday. Expansive banquet facilities and catering service available.*

## STELLA'S CAFÉ
*Restaurant*

If your choice of a place for a wonderful dinner is guided by the credentials of the chef, then Stella's Café is for you. Chef/owner Gregory Hallihan is a graduate, with honors, of the California Culinary Academy (San Francisco), the former sous chef at the popular Willowside Café, with experience at the Ritz Carlton Kannapali, Hawaii. Obviously, he worked hard and learned well. By adding that knowledge to his natural talents in the kitchen, Gregory has created a splendid blend of California Cuisine, with a Pacific Rim/Mediterranean twist to his extremely eclectic menu, which changes every two weeks.

*Stella's Café, 4550 Gravenstein Hwy. N., Sebastopol, CA 95472. Telephone: 707-823-6637. FAX: 707-823-5482. Menu is basically California Cuisine with Pacific Rim and Mediterranean influences. Seats 50. Open six days a week for dinner, starting at 5:30PM. Closed on Tuesdays.*

## SYRAH
*Restaurant*

Syrah may be small, but oh, my! What a lot of brilliantly innovative California-French dishes come out of the compact little kitchen, and how perfectly the wine list complements the menu. One of the youngest restaurants in the county, Syrah is already the first choice for resident and visiting gourmets. Syrah is the first business venture of owner/chef Josh Silvers and his wife Regina, Syrah's president, and they take great delight in expressing their passion for fine food and wine. They are also great communicators, with a highly informative website, where patrons can make reservations on line, sign up for announcements by E-mail and request copies of Varietales - the restaurant newsletter. The menu changes frequently, but because it is the chef's favorite, foie gras is always on the menu in one form or another. To help diners become familiar with lesser-known wine varieties, tasting flights of three different wines are offered. There is a pleasantly varied by-the-glass list as well as a fine selection by-the-bottle.

*Syrah, 205 Fifth St., Santa Rosa, CA 95401. Telephone 707-568-4002. Website: www.syrahbistro.com. There is seating for 60 in the restaurant proper and the elegant indoor courtyard. Open hours are Tuesday through Saturday, with lunch from 11:30AM- 2:30PM and dinner service starting at 5:30PM. Entrée prices range from $18.00 - $25.00. Reservations are requested.*

## TASTINGS RESTAURANT & WINE BAR
*Restaurant*

The building that is now the delightful Tastings Restaurant was originally situated streetside and housed Ned's Burgers, approximately 15-years ago. It was then moved and a dining room was added and it became Mi Ranchito, a popular Mexican restaurant set adjacent to a small shopping center. Now, under the touch of owners Sandy Kim and Derek McCarthy it reflects what Sandy says is "exactly what we look for when we are dining out - great food, wine and a comfortable ambience." Because they enjoy dining al fresco, Sandy and Derek, who is the chef, added a patio. At Tastings, the adventurous diner can make his dining choice from Derek's outstanding a la carte menu and choose a beverage selection from an international wine list. A five-course tasting menu contains suggested companion wines that Sandy and Derek feel enhance their cuisine the best. Another nice touch for those who enjoy a snack or more after the theatre or movies, Tastings virtually has no closing time, but, because the restaurant is small and intimate, it is best to call in advance for reservations. Call for information about Winemaker dinners.

*Tastings Restaurant & Wine Bar, 505 Healdsburg Ave., Healdsburg, CA 95448. Telephone: 707-433-3936, FAX: 707-433-3974. E-mail: derekandsandy@prodigy.net. Website: www.tastingsrestaurant.com. Seating, 30 inside, 7 at counter, 16 on the patio. Open Friday through Monday; lunch 11:30AM - 2:30PM; dinner from 6:00PM.*

## TAVERNA SANTI
*Restaurant*

There is one thing that Thomas Oden, chef and co-owner with chef Franco Dunn of Taverna Santi in Geyserville likes to emphasize about their cheerful, comfortable restaurant: "We have a very extensive menu, which is surprising for a small, rather out-of-the-way establishment. Franco and I love to cook, and it's a great personal pleasure for us to see people's surprise when they find something unexpected on the menu." The concentration is on freshness. The two chefs, both with extensive cooking experience in Sonoma County and abroad, credit their grandmothers as the strongest influence on their culinary choices. They make their own foccacia and pizza dough, their own pasta, salami, pancetta, and smoked ricotta. And, even though they know they can get virtually any ingredient they want at any time of the year, from foreign countries, they use only what is obtainable locally at its peak. Santi, Italian for saints, was also the first name of Santi Catelli, the first restaurateur to serve fine Italian food on the site. The tradition of excellence continues. There is a full bar and a fine wine list, with a generous selection of by-the-glass offerings.

*Taverna Santi, 21047 Geyserville Ave., Geyserville, CA 95441. Telephone: 707-857-1790. FAX: 707-857-1793. E-mail: office@tavernasanti.com. Website: www.tavernasanti.com. Serving lunch, Monday through Saturday, 11:45AM- 2:30PM, dinner nightly 5:30 - 9:00PM. Sitting inside 100, bar seating 30 and patio dining for 100. Reservations Friday and Saturday dinner suggested.*

## UNION HOTEL RESTAURANT, PIZZERIA, SALOON & CAFÉ
*Family Style Restaurant*

The story of the Union Hotel starts in 1925 with the story of Carlo Panizzera, whose descendents still operate the colorful restaurant which traditionally serves such generous portions everyone goes home with great left-overs. Carlo arrived in California in 1917 from Brunia, Italy, and took a job as a cowboy in the San Fernando Valley. When a cousin suggested he move north to the little town of Occidental, he was delighted to leave the heat and rattlesnakes of southern California. When he arrived he bought the Union Saloon, and soon found himself a wonderful wife, who was also a spectacular cook, and the fame of the dining room grew. Additions followed: an outdoor patio, a bakery/café, and, in 1992, a pizzeria. Even as it has grown, nothing much has changed. Mary and Carlo's grandsons, Mark, Dan and Frank Gonnella see to that. There is now a second location: Union Hotel Pizza and Pasta Company, 1007 West College Ave., Santa Rosa, CA 95401.

*Union Hotel Restaurant, Pizzeria, saloon and Café, 3731 Main St., Occidental, CA 95465. Telephone: 707-874-3555. FAX: 707-874-9000. E-mail: info@unionhotel.com. Cuisine is family style Italian. Open hours 11:30AM - 9:00PM, every day except Christmas Eve. Prices, unbelievably moderate.*

## VINEYARDS INN
*Restaurant*

Those dining on the fabulous dishes served up by chef/owner Steve Rose at the Vineyards Inn may not know it but they owe a vote of thanks to Steve's dad, Harry, for the dual emphasis on traditional and popular recipes from both Spain and Mexico. This delightful blend of flavors and ingredients is further enhanced by Steve and Colleen Rose's dedication to their own organic garden, in which they grow most of the perfect-ly ripe produce used in the restaurant. Their devotion to the finest and freshest is particularly noticeable in their mouth-watering seafood specials, their marinated steaks, and succulent local chicken. Long time residents have grown up with tempting lunches and dinners at the Vineyards Inn, which has been serving the hungry in the Sonoma Valley for 20 years.

*The Vineyards Inn, 8445 Sonoma Hwy., Kenwood, CA 95452. Telephone: 707-833-4500. Website: www.vineyardsinn.com. Seats 40 inside and 70 on the enclosed patio. The restaurant serves lunch and dinner. Hours Monday, Wednesday and Thursday, 11:30AM - 9:30PM, Friday and Saturday, 11:30AM - 10:00PM, and Sunday from 11:30AM - 9:00PM.*

## WESTERN BOOT STEAKHOUSE

*Restaurant*

Those who insist that no one eats meat anymore, and others who claim that they can never get a good steak, both need to find their way to the Western Boot Steakhouse. Charbroiled steaks come in sizes from the 8 oz.-Tenderfoot Filet Mignon to the 22 oz.-Top Hand Sirloin. The Western Boot's ribs (spare and beef) appear on platters. Another choice is the combination of a half chicken and spare rib dinner. Diners who visit Western Boot for the first time, learn that they need to arrive good and hungry, even if all they're planning to have is the Barrel Ridin' beef ravioli or the City Slicker's scampi. Owned and operated by the Rochioli family since 1983, Ken Rochioli has preserved the comfortable ranch-hand ambiance with wooden booths and tables and western décor.

*Western Boot Steakhouse, 9 Mitchell Lane, Healdsburg, CA 95448. Telephone: 707-433-6362, FAX: 707-431-2715. Seats 99. Open for lunch, Monday - Friday, 11:30AM - 2:00PM; dinner, 7 days a week, 5:00PM - 10:00PM Friday, 4:00PM - 10:00PM Saturday, 4:00PM - 9:00PM Sunday. Monday through Thursday, 5:00PM - 9:00PM.*

## THE WINEMAKER RESTAURANT

*Restaurant*

If you're one of those who thinks Wienerschnitzel must be a hot dog, then, says Chef/Owner Konrad Weber of The Winemaker Restaurant, a trip to his restaurant is a must! Chef Weber apprenticed in Germany, so learned as a youth how to create the perfect wienerschnitzel. With further training in Switzerland, Holland and England, then considerable cruise line and restaurant experience, Chef Weber increased his cooking repertoire to include specialties from every land he visited. Local favorites are his excellent salmon dishes and roast rack of lamb Provencale, and the beef eaters flock to The Winemaker Friday, Saturday and Sunday evenings for Konrad's Prime Rib, and two with hearty appetites can't find a better bargain than the Chateaubriand Broquetiere - at a remarkable $38.00!

*The Winemaker Restaurant, 875 West Napa St., Sonoma, CA 95476. Telephone: 707-938-8489. Open daily, except Tuesday, 4:30PM - 9:00PM. Seating for 80 patrons. Entrée prices range from $10.00 - $18.00.*

## ZIN RESTAURANT & WINE BAR
*Restaurant*

Time was before nouvelle cuisine, fusion and Tex-Mex that dining out was a simpler activity, and, for those who wanted a good meal at an affordable price, there was usually a friendly neighborhood dining spot, where full meals, called Blue Plate Specials were served nightly. Those who remember those days will be delighted to learn of Zin, where partner/chefs Scott Silva and Jeff Mall have lifted the Blue Plate Special to new heights. As examples of just how fine this offering can be, sample the chicken and dumplings, or buttermilk fried chicken, or gumbo. Jeff is the chef who creates the menus featuring classic American recipes, and Scott is the wine buyer who has put together a wine list featuring the largest selection of Zinfandels in Sonoma county. In case you hadn't guessed, Zin is short for Zinfandel.

*Zin, 344 Center St., Healdsburg, CA 95448.
Telephone: 707-473-0946, FAX 707-473-0642.
Website: www.zinrestaurant.com. Lunch service
Monday, Wednesday Thursday and Friday from
11:30AM - 2:00PM. Dinner nightly from 5:30PM.
Closed Tuesdays. Seating capacity 48, including six
seats at the wine bar.*

TRAVEL NOTES: _____

# Menus

 n a county as well-known for its excellent food sources and outstanding restaurants, it is virtually impossible to supply copies of every menu from every eatery. We have tried here to provide a sampling of the styles of cuisine and the uniqueness of the dining spots. Bon Appetit!

# Dinner at Applewood

Six Tomales Bay Oysters, Three Ways:
On the Halfshell with Lemon and Shallots, Poached in White Wine with Tarragon, Grilled with Garlic Butter  11.00

Ahi Tuna Tartare with Cucumber and Radish Salad, Parsley Cracker and Tomato Sorbet  12.00

Spicy Chilled Curried Carrot Soup with Grappa Soaked Currants,
Toasted Almonds and Fresh and Dried Coriander  8.00

Simple Baby Lettuces in Slow Roasted Shallot Vinaigrette with Shaved Pears and Spiced Pecans  7.00

Lobster and Tomato Terrine in Champagne Gelée with Arugula and Old Balsamic  14.00

Chilled Salad of Grilled Romaine Hearts, Avocado and White Anchovy with Shaved Spanish Table Cheese  10.00

Crisp Maine Crab Fritters with Little Tomatoes, Corn and Grilled Eggplant Purée  11.00

🍎🍎🍎🍎

Roasted Liberty Farms Duck Breast with New England Johnnycakes,
Sweet White Corn and Bing Cherries  24.00

Local Wild King Salmon Grilled with Wild Mushroom and Corn Ragout
in Truffled Mushroom Broth  24.00

Grilled Angus "Rib Eye" Steak with Warm Potato and Watercress Salad,
Garlicky Herb Butter and Fried Garlic Cloves  26.00

Roasted Northern Halibut with Ravioli "Fines Herbes,"
Charred Squash Sauce and Squash Blossom Fritture  23.00

Grilled Tenderloin and Slow Roasted Shoulder of Pork with Chickpea Purée,
Ruby Red Beets and Grilled Nectarines  23.00

🍎🍎🍎🍎

Two Cheeses: One Near, One Far with Black Pepper *Carta Musica* and Ripe Summer Stonefruit  10.00

Pear and Apple "Fougasse" with Orange Flower Crème Fraîche  7.50

Blueberry and Fromage Blanc Cheesecake in Semolina Cookie Crust  7.50

Peach Ice Cream with Almond Fried Dough  7.50

"Assiette Tout Chocolat"  10.00

# Creekside Bistro

## Appetizers

8.50 ~ Warm seafood salad w/ prawns, scallops, halibut bay shrimp. Mixed greens & balsamic vinaigrette.

7.50 ~ Escarots with angel hair pasta.

6.50 ~ Chefs Pâté with baby spinach & Kalamata olives.

6.50 ~ Caesar salad with regiano parmesan

## Entrées

21.00 ~ Hanging Tenderloin of beef w/ black peppercorn sauce. Sauteed mushrooms & french fries.

19.00 ~ Day boat scallops w/ herb beurre blanc sauce & crusty mashed potatoes.

A/a ~ Fresh fish of the day.

18.00 ~ Filet of pork with duxelle of mushrooms & calvados sauce. Served with gratin potatoes.

16.75 ~ Confit of duck with gorgonzola cheese, spinach greens vinaigrette, & roasted yellow finn potatoes.

16.00 ~ Sauteed calf's liver w/ vegetable stir-fry, parisienne potatoes, & balsamic demi-glaze.

15.75 ~ Coq au vin - breast of chicken with red wine demi-glaze & roasted yellow finn potatoes.

*Join us for complimentary wine tasting on Winemaker Fridays, beginning at 6:30 p.m.*

## Salads and Starters

EQUUS CLASSIC TABLESIDE CAESAR SALAD for two or more.  $ 10 per person

STRAWBERRY SALAD honey-balsamic strawberries with spicy greens, sliced red onions,
toasted sesame seeds and shaved pecorino cheese.  $ 7

MIXED SALAD tossed with a Mediterranean blend of lettuces,  summer radishes, a citrus spiked dressing,
then finished with crumbled Redwood Hill teleme cheese and toasted pine nuts.  $ 6

TODAY'S SOUP  $ 5

HOUSE SMOKED SALMON with potato latkes, a red onion remoulade, herb salad, seared fennel and black caviar.  $ 9

HEIRLOOM TOMATO SALAD with Farmstead blue cheese, mint oil, shaved sweet onion and a balsamic reduction.  $ 8

THINLY SLICED PARMA PROSCIUTTO  with grilled asparagus, toasted almonds, shaved Vella asiago pepato cheese,
garnished with sundried tomato gremolata and a drizzle of virgin olive oil.  $ 9

SEARED DUNGENESS CRAB CAKES Two lightly seared cakes with a lemon-caper aioli and preserved lemon slaw.  $ 11

SPICY FRIED CALAMARI Served on a bed of greens with a Provencale salsa and drizzled with a spicy aioli.  $ 11

## Pastas and Risotto

LEMON-CHIVE TAGLIARINI WITH WHITE PRAWNS and toasted garlic, lemon juice, prawn butter, chile flakes,
grana parmesan and wilted arugula.  $ 23          Starter portion  $ 12

TODAY'S RISOTTO SELECTION  Please inquire with your server about today's special risotto.    market price

HERBED PAPPARDELLE PASTA POMODORO with diced roma tomatoes, basil, roasted garlic cloves,
grated smoked mozzarella, grana cheese and basil chiffonade.  $ 15          Starter portion  $ 8

## Entrees

SAUTEED LOBSTER MEDALLIONS cooked tableside by our chef, with potato-leek pancakes, foraged mushrooms,
wilted baby spinach, an apple spiked light cream and finished with a truffled tarragon butter.  $ 33

GRILLED LIBERTY DUCK BREAST with a confit leg, a kashi and wild rice melange, glazed pears,
a lemon-thyme and cherry sauce, sauteed spinach with currants and pine nuts.  $ 27

TODAY'S HAWAIIAN SEAFOOD   Please inquire with your server about today's special seafood entree.    market price

PAN-SEARED WILD SALMON with strawberry risotto,  balsamic drizzle, strawberry coulis, spinach and
balsamic onions.  $ 23

GRILLED 10-OUNCE PORK CHOP with Yukon gold puree, roasted red onions, fennel wedges, sunburst squash,
bell peppers and tomatoes with a light porcini mushroom cream.  $ 21

WOOD-FIRED CHICKEN BREAST  with wild summer mushrooms, wild rice, creamed leeks, chicken glace and our special
house wilted spinach.  $ 20

CK RANCH LAMB LOIN CHOPS WOOD-GRILLED with crushed coriander potatoes, a fig and balsamic sauce,
toasted pine nuts, French  and yellow wax beans.  $ 29

## Steak Selections

GRILLED 7-OUNCE  FILET  MIGNON          or          12-OUNCE DRY-AGED NEW YORK STEAK          $ 29
Both steaks are served with a bacon-onion sauce, roasted new potatoes, house wilted spinach,
foie gras butter and a grilled red onion salad.

MIXED GRILL Portions of petit filet mignon, Caggiano's chorizo, rich and tender west Texas antelope chop served
with grilled vegetables and fingerling potatoes.  $ 28

### Doug V. Lane, Executive Chef

## Jellyfish Entrées

Wok Charred Wild Salmon Lemon-Ginger Sauce, Jasmine
Rice, Baby Bok Choy, Toasted Ginger $18.

Steamed Bass & Asian Aromatics w/ Julienne of Snow Peas
Carrots & Potatoes w/ Soy Ginger Sesame Oil & Rice $22

Lobster Coconut Tempura w/ Lime Aioli, Mango Salsa, &
Sweet Pearl Rice & Lop Cheong Wrapped in Banana
Leaves $29

Spit Roasted Sonoma Chicken, Garlic Chive Jus,
Gai Lan Broccoli, Yukon Gold Whipped Potatoes $20.

Star Anise Petaluma Liberty Duck Breast w/ Cherry Berry
Sauce, Braised Napa Cabbage & Potato Galette Napoleon $24

Lemongrass & Toasted Coriander Seed Crusted Pork Loin
Cutlets w/ Green Thai Curry Sauce, Rice Noodles $22

House Smoked C K Ranch Lamb Loin Chop w/ Long
Beans, Roasted Elephant Garlic Custard, Black Olive Jus $28

Grilled New York Steak & Miso Braised Beef Short Rib,
Smoked Exotic Mushrooms, Grilled Asparagus &
Crisp Maui Onions $26

Shiitake Mushroom Ravioli, Local Spinach,
Barbequed Eggplant, Charred Tomato Broth $17

Side of Mashed Potatoes or Rice $3
For parties of more than 6 an 18% gratuity will be added to
your bill

Executive Chef – Barbara Hom
Chef de Cuisine – Tim Horrock

## APPETIZERS & SMALL PLATES

**OUR HOUSE SOUP,** GUAJILLO CHILI AND ROASTED TOMATO WITH SMOKED CHICKEN . . . . . . . . . . . . . . . . . . . . . . . . . .5.00

**SOUP OF THE DAY** . . . . . . . . . . . . . . . . . . . . . . . . . . . . . . . . . . . . . . . . . . . . . . . . . . .5.00

**HOUSE SALAD,** SONOMA ORGANIC GREENS, CHOICE OF BALSAMIC VINAIGRETTE, GORGONZOLA WALNUT DRESSING
OR NAVARRO VER JUS VINAIGRETTE . . . . . . . . . . . . . . . . . . . . . . . . . . . . . . . . . . . . . . 6.00

**HEARTS OF ROMAINE SALAD,** CAESAR STYLE DRESSING, GARLIC CROUTONS, DRY AGED JACK CHEESE  SMALL . . . . . . . 7.00
LARGE . . . . . . . 9.00

**GRILLED PEAR SALAD** WITH SONOMA GREENS, ENDIVE, WALNUTS, GORGONZOLA AND AN AGED BALSAMIC DRESSING . . . . 8.00

**WILTED SPINACH SALAD** WITH GRILLED PORTABELLA MUSHROOM, ROASTED RED ONION, APPLEWOOD SMOKED BACON,
REDWOOD HILL FARMS CHEVRE AND AGED RED WINE VINAIGRETTE . . . . . . . . . . . . . . . . . . . . . . . . . . . . . . . . .9.75

### CALIFORNIA CHEESE PLATE
WITH DRIED FRUIT CHUTNEY AND TOASTED WALNUTS OR HONEY AND ROASTED HAZELNUTS

**CHOICE OF CHEESE**
POINT REYES ORIGINAL BLUE FROM FARMSTEAD CHEESE COMPANY
BELLWETHER FARMS CARMODY
JOE MATOS ST. GEORGE
SMALL......7.00
LARGE.....10.00

**GRILLED CAJUN PRAWNS** SPICED WITH SOME KICK, WITH CREOLE-STYLE REMOULADE AND SAFFRON RICE.
SEASONED MILDLY ON REQUEST . . . . . . . . . . . . . . . . . . . . . . . . . . . . . . . . . . . . . . . . . . . . 9.95

**SEARED SEA OF CORTEZ SCALLOP** WITH POTATO PUREE, CAVIAR AND CHIVE OIL . . . . . . . . . . . . . . . . . . . . . . . 12.00

**OYSTERS ON THE ½ SHELL** WITH CHAMPAGNE WASABI MIGNONETTE . . . . . . . . . . . . . . . . . . . 1.95 EACH - 6 FOR 10.00

**GRILLED OYSTERS** WITH ROASTED TOMATO SALSA & DRY JACK CHEESE . . . . . . . . . . . . . . . . . . . 2.50 EACH - 6 FOR 13.00

**PEI MUSSELS** WITH PERNOD, FENNEL, JALAPEÑO AND DILL BROTH. . . . . . . . SERVED WITH GRILLED GARLIC BREAD . . . . . 9.00

**AHI TUNA TARTAR,** PARSLEY SHALLOT VINAIGRETTE, PICKLED CUCUMBER, FRIED LEEKS AND A CITRUS COULIS. . . . . . . . 9.95

**BASIL FETTUCCINE WITH SMOKED CHICKEN,** NIÇOISE OLIVES, POACHED GARLIC AND SUN DRIED TOMATOES . . . . 11.00
LARGE. . . . . . 15.00

**MIXX HOUSE MADE SAUSAGE PLATE** WITH BRIOCHE BRUSCHETTA, FRESH MOZZARELLA, OLIVE TAPENADE,
TOMATO CHUTNEY AND BASIL OIL . . . . . . . . . . . . . . . . . . . . . . . . . . . . . . . . . . . . . . . . . . . . 9.95

### Appetizers – suitable for sharing

| | |
|---|---|
| "Snacks": House-cured salmon, chilled prawns, ham, housemade crackers, more | 10.75 |
| Pizza "Pontchartrain" – Andouille sausage, peppers, onions, Creole sauce, and parmesan cheese | 9.75 |
| Pizza with mushrooms, Mezzosecco cheese, garlic, sage and spinach | 9.75 |
| Fried shrimp, scallops, and calamari with malt-vinegar mignonette and Creole tartar sauce | 10.75 |
|    –recommended with "J" Sparkling $8.50 | |

### Soups, Salads, Etc.

| | Starter | Entrée |
|---|---|---|
| Gazpacho, New Mexico-style | 4.00 | 6.00 |
| Chowder of sea bass with bacon and housemade crackers | 4.75 | 7.00 |
| Spicy crab-and-fish cakes with tartar sauce and jicama-cabbage slaw | 9.75 | 13.75 |
| Shrimp and crab Louis on avocado and field greens | 10.75 | 13.75 |
| 'Sassy' Caesar - Romaine leaves, Wisantigo parmesan, sourdough croutons, tapenade | 5.75 | 9.75 |
| Green Salad, Shaker-style | | |
| Boston lettuce, Blue Lake beans, tarragon-mustard vinaigrette, shaved onion, fresh herbs | 4.75 | |
|   with "Buttermilk" blue cheese | 5.50 | |
| Redwood Hill crottin goat cheese in pastry with lemon-herb green sauce, tomatoes and baby spinach | 9.75 | 14.75 |
|   –recommended with 1999 Quivira Sauvignon Blanc $6.50 | | |
| "Meatloaf Sandwich with ketchup and mustard" | | |
| Bourbon-laced venison and pork terrine with dried-cherry ketchup, whole-grain mustard and toasts | 8.75 | |
|   –recommended with 2000 Joseph Swan Pinot Noir $7.50 | | |

### Hot Dishes

| | Starter | Entrée |
|---|---|---|
| Herb-rice croquette, black bean mousse, griddled cheddar grits, two sauces, braised greens | 7.50 | 11.25 |
| Fresh fettucine with white cheddar, parmesan, corn, cherry tomatoes, snap peas | 6.50 | 10.75 |
| King salmon and diver scallops with orange-ancho chile butter sauce and green rice porridge | 9.75 | 16.50 |
| Rare yellowfin tuna wrapped in smoked ham with sweet pepper-green olive relish and vinaigrette dressed vegetables | 9.75 | 16.75 |
|   –recommended with 2001 Raptor Ridge Pinot Gris $5.75 | | |
| Grilled pork tenderloin with apple-bing cherry demi glace | 9.00 | 15.00 |
|   –recommended with 2000 Amity Gamay Noir $4.75 | | |
| Braised leg of Central Valley Muscovy duck with dried figs, olives and pinot noir | | 14.75 |
|   –recommended with 2000 Willakenzie Pinot Noir $8.50 | | |
| Pot roast of CK lamb with zinfandel-herb jus and garlic mashed potatoes | | 15.75 |
|   –recommended with 2000 Seghesio Zinfandel $6.50 | | |
| Strip loin steak of Montana beef with port wine jus, blue cheese, bacon and creamed spinach | | 19.50 |
|   –recommended with 1999 Eaglepoint Ranch Syrah $8.00 | | |

Scott Snyder, Chef
Christian Meise, Sous chef

# SONOMA-MERITAGE
# OYSTER BAR
707-938-9430

## The Raw

### Oysters on Half shell
| | |
|---|---|
| Hog Island (local)M | $1.85 |
| Bluepoint (Northeast)M | $1.60 |
| Fanny Bay (Washington)Lg | $1.60 |
| Pearl point (Washington)Sm | $1.60 |

Sampler platter (2 of each kind) $12

### Clams
| | |
|---|---|
| Littleneck clams | $1.50 |

### Ceviche of the day
| | |
|---|---|
| Ask your schucker | $8.50 |

## And the Cooked

### Jumbo Shrimp cocktail
| | |
|---|---|
| Jumbo Gulf Shrimp (6ea) | $12 |

### Mussels
| | |
|---|---|
| Steamed mussels (½lb) | $7 |

### Clams
| | |
|---|---|
| Manilla clams in buttter garlic broth | $8 |

### Maine lobster
| | |
|---|---|
| Half | $15 |
| Whole | $30 |

### Dungeness crab
| | |
|---|---|
| Half | $15 |
| Whole | $30 |

| | |
|---|---|
| Oysters Rockerfeller | $11 |
| Oysters Casino | $11 |
| Littleneck Clams Casino | $11 |

**Seafood platter $40**
½ Cracked Dungeness crab
Ceviche of the Day
Oysters on the half shell(4)
Jumbo Gulf Shrimp (4)
Chilled Steamed mussels(6)
Littleneck clams on the half shell (4)

**Big seafood platter $60**
½ Cracked Dungeness crab
½ Cracked Maine lobster
Ceviche of the Day
Jumbo Gulf Shrimp (6)
Chilled Steamed mussels (8)
Littleneck clams on the half shell(6)
Oysters on the half shell(8)

**Jumbo seafood platter $90**
Cracked Dungeness crab
Cracked Maine lobster
Ceviche of the Day
Jumbo Gulf Shrimp (9)
Chilled Steamed mussels (12)
Littleneck clams on the half shell(9)
Oysters on the half shell(12)

Condiments
Spicy Cocktail sauce, Remoulade,
Champagne migonette

# Tastings

### Coromandel Oysters
with Fried Leeks, Wasabi Tobiko Caviar & Champagne Mignonette
NV Grandin Brut, Ingrandes-sur-Loire

. . . . . . .

### Butter Poached Maine Lobster
in an Heirloom Tomato & Lobster Broth with Watercress & Basil Oil
01 Davis Bynum Fume Blanc, Shone Farm, Russian River Valley

. . . . . . .

### Pan seared Striped Bass
with Fennel Custard, Baby Spinach & Balsamic Reduction
00 Bouchard Le Chamville Mâcon Villages, Burgundy

. . . . . . .

### Roasted stuffed Boneless Quail
on Braised Escarole & Caramelized Onions with Black Plum Sauce
99 Chateau Saint Esteve D'Uchaux, Côtes du Rhône Villages

. . . . . . .

### Blueberry Crêpe
with Vanilla Ice Cream, Blueberry Sauce & Chocolate Truffle

5-Course Tastings 49
Wine Pairings add 15

Chef/Owner Derek McCarthy

Lodging

hen the day's adventures are over, there's nothing that beckons quite so invitingly as a room or suite of one's own. Then it's time to kick off the shoes, prop up the feet and savor the amenities to be found in hotels and inns of varying sizes and styles throughout Sonoma County. Even in the smallest, least pretentious settings, a hair dryer, ironing board and iron, whirlpool tub, and, of course TV with VCR will be found. Videos, books and games are nearly omni-present, and fluffy towels, robes and a mint on the pillow are de rigeur. For those seeking respite from the work-a-day world, there are also havens with no TV, no phone and no computer access, where the beeping of a cell phone is blessedly absent. No matter how you prefer to rest, you'll find the perfect setting, from ultra-modern chain hotels, to rustic cabins, restored Victorians and simple campgrounds under the redwoods.

Whatever your choice, there is one absolute certainty in Sonoma County - there will be a superb breakfast to start your day, a glass of wine to greet you when you return from your wanderings or tea and cookies on the veranda.

Two words of warning - plan ahead. During the harvest season (September through November) and at the height of the summer, make reservations a month or even two in advance. On the weekends which feature a major event like the Harvest Fair, Passport Day, Sonoma Showcase or the Sonoma Valley Auction, any place to lay your head may be a trifle hard to find. A three-month lead time then, may not be too preposterous. (See Events for dates). Note, too, that bed and breakfast inns almost universally require a two-night stay (Friday and Saturday or Saturday and Sunday) except in the slower winter months.

With the wealth of comfortable places to stay in Sonoma County, it is impossible to mention them all, so, what follows is a mere sampling. The Chamber of Commerce offices in any of Sonoma County's cities can help with suggestions in their areas.

## APPLEWOOD INN & RESTAURANT

Constructed in 1922 as the family home of wealthy Santa Rosans, Ralph and Gretchen Belden, the stunning house with its 60-acre apple orchard was later transformed into a bed and breakfast inn called The Estate. When Jim Caron and Darryl Notter purchased the property in 1985 they continued to operate the inn for another ten years. By 1995, they had renamed the site Applewood Inn & Restaurant, which they felt was more in keeping with its historic past. A year later they began a renovation designed to recreate the ambiance of the country home and gentleman's farm that it once was. By 1999 they had completed their plans to add two Mediterranean-style villas, and to incorporate the look of the Beldens' apple barn in a new, larger, more distinctive restaurant. There are 19 stylish rooms and suites in the two villas, set under the redwoods in the quiet and seclusion of Pocket Canyon, Guerneville. Each of the inn's rooms is individually decorated, with sinfully comfy queen size beds, Egyptian cotton towels and fine hand-pressed linens. Guests enjoy a full breakfast and two cozy retreats: the solarium and library sitting room. Garden tours are encouraged, and when the guests depart their hosts urge them to take along some of the bounty from the garden. (See also Dining)

*Applewood Inn & Restaurant, 13555 Highway 116, Guerneville, CA 95446. Telephone 707-869-9093, FAX: 707-869-9170. E-mail: stay@aplewoodinn.com. Website: www.applewoodinn.com. 19 rooms, restaurant. Rates: $155.00 - $295.00.*

## BELLE DE JOUR INN

Small and enchanting Belle de Jour is a picturesque hideaway on a hillside at the north end of Healdsburg. The property was part of the original Sotoyome Rancho and the main house, where innkeepers Tom and Brenda Hearn reside, is a single story Italianate built around 1873. The country kitchen in the Hearns' home is a charming setting for a bountiful breakfast served to the guests each morning. The four white, wood frame gabled cottages and Carriage House are 1970s in their architecture, but Twenty-first Century in every other respect. For the comfort and convenience of the guests, all accommodations have private entrances, gas fireplaces, air conditioning, ceiling fans, refrigerators, telephones, AM/FM radios and CD/Tape players. King units have whirlpool tubs for two; queen units have steam showers or single whirlpool tub. Sun-dried sheets, robes for guest use and fresh flowers in each room are just some of the nicer touches. All beds are king or queen sized with down comforters and pillows. The inn is totally non-smoking, and a two-night minimum is required on weekends.

*Belle de Jour Inn, 16276 Healdsburg Ave., Healdsburg, CA 95448. Telephone: 707-431-9777, FAX: 707-431-7412. Website: www.belledejourinn.com. Four cottages and The Carriage House Suite. Rates: $185.00 - $300.00, confirmed by one night advance deposit.*

## CALDERWOOD INN

The romantic Calderwood Inn, a lovely Queen Anne Victorian, was built in 1902 by the John Miller family, prominent local fruit growers and processors. It is constructed entirely of first growth redwood and is surrounded by lush rose gardens, koi ponds, fountains and ancient redwood, cedar and cypress trees. In the restoration of the inn, great care was given to preserving the estate's landscaping, much of it designed and planted by the famed horticulturist, Luther Burbank, a close friend of the Miller family. Two broad porches, with traditional wicker furnishings are ideal for relaxation, catching up on books, or plotting the day's visits to nearby wineries, antique shops and points of historical interest. Hosts Paul and Jennifer Zawodny will be happy to make reservations for tours, dining out, local events or a pampering hour or two at a spa. There are six rooms, all with private baths. Some of the suites have fireplaces, others have large, luxurious whirlpool tubs. Each day at Calderwood starts with a full breakfast, and visitors are welcomed back from the day's adventuring with appetizers, and late night dessert.

*Calderwood Inn, 25 West Grant St., Healdsburg, CA 95448. Telephone: 707-431-1110. Website: www.calderwoodinn.com. Rates: $145.00 - $235.00. First night's deposit required when making reservations.*

## CAMELLIA INN

While a good many of the bed and breakfast inns in Sonoma County have a certain historical significance, few tell as illustrious a story as does Camellia Inn. Built in 1869 by Ransome Powell, a pioneer resident of the brand new town, it was purchased by the Seawell family, whose son, J. Walter, established his medical offices in the family home after graduating from the University of California. Later he turned the dwelling into Healdsburg's first hospital. Concerned with the well-being of the spirit, as well as the body, young Seawell, through the good offices of his friend Luther Burbank, received and planted a number of spectacular camellias on the inn's grounds. In 1981, Del and Ray Lewand, escapees from Los Angeles smog and traffic, purchased the residence. and turned it into the present inn. The home was in such excellent condition, with its fine inlaid hardwood floors, graceful chandeliers, and decorative friezes, that few changes or improvements were necessary. The furnishings are antiques, true to the era, and the showpieces of the inn are the twin marble fireplaces and the ornate mahogany overmantle in the dining room.

New camellias, restoration of a 1920s tiled fish pond complete with brightly colored carp and a tiled swimming pool under the oaks add to the enjoyment of a stay. Each of the nine thoughtfully appointed rooms features a private bath and blissfully comfortable beds, dressed in soft bed linens. Guests at Camellia Inn start the day with a breakfast of fresh fruit, juice, homemade baked goodies and preserves, cereal, French bread and a main breakfast dish. There is a social hour in the early evening with local refreshments, which may include Ray's own wines, since the inn is also a bonded winery - Camellia Cellars.

*Camellia Inn, 211 North St., Healdsburg, CA 95448. Telephone: 707-433-8182, FAX: 707-433-8130. E-mail: info@camelliainn.com. Website: www.camelliainn.com. Nine rooms. Rates: $99.00 - $209.00.*

## DOUBLETREE HOTEL

To greet the new millennium, the Doubletree Hotel completed its $8 million renovation project and threw the doors open on new rooms, expanded public meeting space and a first-class restaurant. Everything is fresh and exciting, from the first glimpse of the Mission-style buildings, with their buff-pink walls and ruddy red-tiled roofs, to the broad lawns, sparkling pool, handsomely equipped exercise room and the gracious welcome with the trademark chocolate chip cookie. There are 245 spacious rooms and suites, with all the amenities, including valet and room service, coffee makers, hairdryers, irons and ironing boards. Attention to the comfort of their guests starts long before they arrive, with the complimentary Sonoma County airport courtesy van. For those arriving by car, there is ample free on-site parking.  Meeting planners are presented with

a "Meeting Planner Guarantee" assuring no glitches, no disappointments. Bacchus Restaurant and Wine Bar chef, Eric McCutcheon lends his inimitable touches to what he calls Sonoma Cuisine, relying on wonderfully fresh products from local farmers and purveyors to lend a note of distinction to his breakfast, lunches and dinners. Restaurant service is open early (6:00 a m) and late (10:00 p m) to accommodate its patrons.

*Doubletree Hotel, One Doubletree Drive, Rohnert Park, CA 94928. Telephone: 707-584-5466, FAX: 707- 586-9726. Website: www.doubletreehotels.com. 245 rooms. Rates range from $99.00 - $159.00, November through April; $119.00 - $249.00, May through October. Hilton Honor points and other airline partner points accepted.*

## DRY CREEK INN (BEST WESTERN)

Wine tourists couldn't ask for a better location when planning visits to the Dry Creek Valley and Alexander Valley than the Dry Creek Inn. The inn lies right between these two premium wine appellations. Spacious rooms and executive suites are designed with the business traveler in mind. The custom executive mini-suites feature special desks with electrical outlets, telephone with dataport, swivel chair and oversized TV. Rooms are provided for both smokers and non-smokers, with king or double queen beds, refrigerators, in-room coffee service and a welcome gift bottle of wine. A complimentary Continental breakfast is served each morning. No need to miss out on your fitness routine while you travel, Dry Creek Inn has an excellent pool, spa and fitness center. A sister hotel, Sonoma Valley Inn, is located in the city of Sonoma to the east.

*Dry Creek Inn, 198 Dry Creek,, Rd., Healdsburg, CA 95448. Telephone: 707-433-0300, FAX: 707-433-129. E-mail: drycreekin@aol.com. Website: www.drycreekinn.com. 103 rooms. Rates: $89.00 - $179.00. AAA approved. Senior, group and corporate rates available. Two-night minimum applies to all special event and holiday weekends.*

## DU CHAMP HOTEL

When Peter and Pat Lenz, former owners of the four-star restaurant, "A Moveable Feast" in the Hamptons, and founders of Lenz Winery on Long Island, moved from the Napa Valley to Healdsburg in the mid-1990s, their plan was to build a small hotel. On a unique, downtown property, straddling Foss Creek, they created a contemporary European style hotel - the Duchamp - with six villas and four artist cottages in a serene garden setting surrounding the 50-foot lap pool and spa. The hotel reflects the witty, avant-garde flavor of Marcel Duchamp, the 20th Century artist whose work influenced the development of Surrealism, Dada and Pop Art. All of the cottages are contemporary in decor, with every modern amenity and custom-built furnishings designed by Pat Lenz. In the morning, a healthful breakfast of Downtown Bakery pastries, granola, seasonal fruit and artisanal cheese is served by the pool. In the afternoons, Peter Lenz oversees the Wine Bar where personally selected local wines, as well as Duchamp Sparkling Wine, the hotel's personal cuvee from Iron Horse Vineyards, are available.

*Duchamp Hotel, 421 Foss St., Healdsburg, CA 95448. Telephone: 707-431-1300, FAX: 707-431-1333 Website: www.duchamphotel.com. Rates $225.00 - $375.00. Reservations required.*

## FARMHOUSE INN

The name "The Farmhouse" could just be a quaint attention-getting device, but it isn't. The Farmhouse Inn's birth dates back to 1873, and after a complete renovation, it opened as a full service inn in 1990. Most recently San Francisco designer, Cheryl Gordon of KK Architects has worked closely with the proprietors to develop an elegant English/French country style for the eight cottages and the events center. The owners themselves trace their lineage almost as far back as the original farm buildings. Siblings Catherine and Joe Bartolomei, are fourth generation Russian River vineyard owners, and along with their father, Lee, and step-brother Mike Tommervik are dedicated to the preservation and promotion of Sonoma County's diverse agricultural heritage. The Farmhouse combines the best elements of warm Sonoma County hospitality, scrumptious food, fine wine and luxurious accommodations. Each cottage features such amenities as wood burning fireplaces, feather beds, two person whirlpool tubs, saunas, luxurious toiletries, sensuous linens, TVs, VCRs, CD players and refrigerators. Breakfast is served each morning in the morning room, overlooking the gardens. Thursday through Sunday evenings, Chef Stephen Litke prepares his signature cuisine, matched with a wine list showcasing many of the finest wines of Sonoma County and a coffee menu with some of the world's best brews. The grounds are an idyllic blend of elegant gardens, rugged woods, picturesque vineyards, fountains and a pool for leisurely lounging

*The Farmhouse, 7871 River Rd., Forestville, CA 95436. Telephone 707-887-3300, FAX: 707-887-3311. Website: www.farmhouseinn.com. Eight cottages. Rates: $160.00 - $275.00.*

## FERN GROVE COTTAGES

The daylight hours at Fern Grove Cottages offer a plethora of options: relax by the swimming pool, walk into entrancing downtown Guerneville for shopping or dining, hike or picnic in Armstrong Redwoods State Park, or make the short drive to explore wineries, check out the produce at growers' fields along the Farm Trails, or drive to the coast and dip a toe into the mighty Pacific. There's golfing, tennis and horseback riding nearby and a wide number of spots to put a canoe or kayak into the Russian River. The 21 cottages at Fern Grove Cottages are classic 1920s architecture, in a mix of studios and one and two bedroom units, with original knotty pine interiors, wood burning fireplaces, double whirlpool tubs and private decks. Hosts Mike and Margaret Kennett are also animal friendly and will welcome good natured pets by prior arrangement. A generous and tasty breakfast buffet greets guests each morning.

*Fern Grove Cottages, 16650 Highway 116, Guerneville, CA 95446. Telephone: 707-869-8105, FAX: 707-869-1615. E-mail: innkeepers@ferngrove.com. Website: www.ferngrove.com. Rates: $79.00 - $219.00.*

## FLAMINGO RESORT HOTEL

Built in 1957, the Flamingo Resort Hotel & Conference Center enjoys historic landmark status. The property includes 170 spacious rooms and suites with an exceptional new business class wing called the Courtyard. The hotel lobby, Terrace Grill restaurant and Cabaret Lounge have been elegantly remodeled, and the restaurants provide full-service meals and entertainment seven days a week for hotel guests and day visitors. Among the hotel's special features is its extensive amount of conference space, a serene garden area with a 25-meter heated swimming pool and outdoor spa and the world-class Montecito Heights Health & Racquet Club. The spa offers more than 30 beauty and body treatments designed to reduce stress and reestablish health and balance.

*Flamingo Resort Hotel & Conference Center, 2777 Fourth St., Santa Rosa, CA 95405. Telephone: 800-848-8300 or 707-545-8530. FAX: 707-568-0442. E-mail: info@flamingoresort.com. Website: www.flamingoresort.com.*

## FORT ROSS LODGE

Rolling dunes, capped with sturdy grasses, floating clouds, fishing boats arriving, heavy with their catch, beaches and cliffs - these are the surroundings for those adventurers traveling Coast Highway 1. One of the best and most comfortable spots to stay when visiting this whale and bird watchers paradise is at Fort Ross Lodge, established in the 1980s by the Romeo family, who still welcome their guests with old-fashioned hospitality. Fort Ross Lodge lies just 12 miles north of Jenner. Just about ten miles farther north is Fort Ross State Park, where the daily life of the Russian settlers who arrived in 1812, is reenacted each day. There are 22 rooms at the Lodge with dramatic views of the ocean, cozy fireplaces, TVs, VCRs, refrigerators and private patios with barbecues. A central area with sauna and hot tub offers a luxurious way to take in the views while enjoying total relaxation.

There are also several units which include a private hot tub on the patio or in room whirlpool tubs and saunas.

*Fort Ross Lodge, 20705 Coast Hwy. 1, Jenner, CA 95450. Telephone: 707-847-3333, FAX: 707-847-3330. Website: www.fortrosslodge.com. Rates $78.00 - $225.00, double occupancy. No pets are allowed.*

## FOUNTAINGROVE INN

In designing the Fountaingrove Inn, the architects were faced with a strong challenge - to achieve a suitable manner of integrating powerful historic forces with modern expectations. The land on which the inn sits was the site of the spiritual community of Thomas Lake Harris, self-proclaimed "Father and Pivot and Primate and King of the Brotherhood of the New Life." The name Fountaingrove referred to the abundant springs in the hills above Harris' fairytale mansion, with its grand staircase, magnificent ballroom and a 10,000 book library. Among the charismatic Harris' beliefs was faith in the health-giving and spiritually uplifting properties of fine wine. To supply an abundant source, he built a winery and planted his property with vineyards and soon had earned a reputation for prize-winning wines under his Fountain Grove label. The remaining structure on the estate, the Round Barn, once used as an equestrian center, still stands. In designing the buildings of Fountaingrove Inn, the profile of the buildings was kept deliberately low, sweeping across the land to afford an unobscured view of the landmark Round Barn. This same simple elegance characterizes the inn's 126 rooms. They are almost Oriental in their simplicity, with polished brass appointments, mirrored walls and graceful details. Each unit includes stereo television, double closets and work spaces with modem jacks to fill the needs of the traveling businessman. Each morning a newspaper is placed at the door and a complimentary buffet is set out each morning in the inn's restaurant, Equus. There are banquet and meeting facilities, and special discounts are offered to government employees, seniors and large groups.

*Fountaingrove Inn, 101 Fountaingrove Parkway, Santa Rosa, CA 95401. Telephone: Telephone 707-578-6101. FAX: 707-544-3126. Website: www.fountaingrove.com. Rates: $149.00 - $299.00*

## THE GABLES WINE COUNTRY INN

It's not uncommon to find an energetic, creative young couple who have fled from the freeways and smog of Southern California to find a new life amid the vines and hillsides of Sonoma County. Judy and Michael Ogne were one such couple, seeking a country environment and a pleasant way to make a living for themselves and their two daughters. When they found The Gables, it was almost as if they had come home, even though the handsome building had been long neglected. They started renovation of the interior first, and as soon as one room was as beautiful and comfortable as they could make it, they started welcoming guests. One by one the seven rooms were brought back to their former glory, then Michael and daughter Jennifer spent an entire summer scraping, restoring and painting the outside. They chose the five colors for the exterior that permitted the Inn to be an official "painted lady" of San Francisco Victorian fame. So perfect was the recreation

that The Gables was placed on the National Register of Historic Places. There is more to the story and the Ognes are happy to relate tales about the original owners, William and Mary Roberts, for whom the private cottage on the grounds is named. A good time for the story telling is around the breakfast table while enjoying a multi-course gourmet breakfast or in the afternoon over a cup of tea. The seven rooms are designed to a style of decor that harmonizes with the room's name and the William and Mary's Cottage – separate and private – has a wood stove, kitchenette, queen size bed in a loft bedroom, whirlpool tub for two, TV, VCR and a private phone line with dataport. All rooms have private baths and all the amenities to make the guest's stay memorable.

*The Gables Wine Country Inn, 4257 Petaluma Hill Rd., Santa Rosa, CA 95404. Telephone: 707-585-7777, 800-422-5376, FAX: 707-584-5634. Website: www.thegablesinn.com. 7 rooms and a private cottage. Rates: $175.00 - $250.00. On weekends the reservation is two nights. During harvest and on special events weekends, the minimum stay is three nights.*

## GAIGE HOUSE INN

One of the lovely features which has given Gaige House Inn its reputation as "a star in the Valley of the Moon," is the exotic array of gardens which surround the inn and pool. In the handsomely landscaped creekside area there is a classic and traditional rose garden, perennial gardens with tropical grasses and an herb and vegetable garden which supplies many of the fresh elements of the full two-course breakfasts served each morning. All the rooms have queen or king size beds, private baths, phones, robes and American toiletries. Some rooms have whirlpool baths, fireplaces or Japanese style soaking tubs. Gaige House, an 1890 Queen Ann Italianate building was completely renovated in the early 1980s and a second face lift was completed between 1997 and 2001. The interior decor is

ters with two queen beds. Extra amenities include computer hook-ups in all rooms, hair dryers, an iron and ironing board and, right outside the door, a year round swimming pool and hot tub. A complimentary Continental breakfast is served each morning in the lounge, which is the perfect spot to plan the day's explorations. Local newspapers are available and a rack of brochures describing scenic and recreational attractions, nearby wineries and events make preparing an itinerary a pleasant task. For family reunions or a corporate meeting, Geyserville Inn has a small private conference room, a beautifully landscaped lawn and gazebo area. The Hoffman House Wine Country Deli, officiated over by Chef Dan Lucia, is just steps away to supply the makings for a great picnic, or arrange a small dinner party.

sophisticated, with Asian and Indonesian influences over a restrained California simplicity. The inn is a non-smoking property, and pets are not allowed.

*Gaige House Inn, 13540 Arnold Dr., Glen Ellen, CA 95442. Telephone: 707-935-0237, FAX: 707-935-6411. Website: www.gaige.com. 15 rooms and suites, at rates from $150.00 - $550.00*

*The Geyserville Inn, 21714 Geyserville Ave., Geyserville, CA 95441. Telephone: 707-857-4343, FAX: 707-857-4411. Website: www.geyservilleinn.com. Rates $87.00 - 4164.00, which change seasonally.*

## GEYSERVILLE INN

For a wine maven with a serious yen to live in the wine country, amid the vines, with a hot tub to soak in, fine wines at hand and unmatched dining, but with a limited amount of cash, the place to indulge his/her fantasy is The Geyserville Inn. The inn has everything, particularly location. It's right in the heart of the lush Alexander Valley, with premium grapes growing all around and hillside views in all directions. When it comes to comfort, it's as if Dan Christensen, the inn owner, and his sons Dan, Jr. and Robert invented the word. There are king or queen size beds in each of the 38 rooms, with two more spacious quar-

## HEALDSBURG COUNTRY GARDENS

When you call to make a reservation at Healdsburg Country Gardens, you are not just getting a splendid room with all the little extras, you are going to be staying in your own little house - the Country Cottage, ideal for two, a Country Home, comfortable for four to six, with all the necessities including a dishwasher, or the Country Farmhouse, ideal for up to six amiable people, that even has its own washer and dryer, and fully equipped kitchen. It's the perfect getaway from the work-a-day world. When you awake in the morning at Healdsburg Country Gardens you are certain to be greeted by birdsong, in a great chorus from the two aviaries filled with canaries, cockatiels and finches. The property on which these enchanting cottages sit is a former 25-acre prune ranch. The old dehydrator is where hosts Barbara and Walt Gruber now store their wine. Another touch of history is the old barn which was built in 1902 and survived the 1906 earthquake just fine. The original Victorian home was dismantled in the 1940s, and the wood was used to build two of the smaller homes.

*Healdsburg Country Gardens, 670 Bailhache Ave., Healdsburg, CA 95448. Telephone: 707-431-8630, FAX: 707-431-8639. E-mail: info@hcountrygardens.com. Website: www.hcountrygardens.com. Rates $125 - $300.00 per night. Weekend rates slightly higher. Monthly rates available December through April.*

## HEALDSBURG INN ON THE PLAZA

The entrance to Healdsburg Inn on the Plaza is through Innpressions, a gallery of remarkable art, most of it by local artists. Dyanne Celi, daughter of Inn owner Genny Jenkins, presides over the gallery, checks in the guests, offers FAX and copier service and tells the story of the Inn's former life as the F. A. Kruse building which, at various times, housed dental parlors, a shoe store and a bank. The guest suites, on two floors, have either king or queen-size beds and all have fireplaces, TV, VCR, and telephone. Furnishings are comfortably Victorian and the baths are well-proportioned and stocked with all the amenities. Right in the heart of town, the windows of the guest suites overlook the Plaza and the passing parade of strollers and sightseers. Guests are treated to a full breakfast in the solarium/dining room, champagne brunch on Saturday and Sunday, and wine refreshment each afternoon.

*Healdsburg Inn on the Plaza, 110 Matheson St., Healdsburg, CA 95448. Telephone: 707-433-6991 or 800-431-8663, FAX:707-433-9513. E-mail: innpressions@earthlink.net. Website: www.healdsburginn.com. Weekend rates, $255.00 - $285.00 per night. Mid-week discounts available.*

## HOLIDAY INN EXPRESS HOTEL & SUITES

A stay at the Holiday Inn Express Hotel & Suites, in Sebastopol, gives the traveler a glimpse of the quieter, more bucolic and tranquil beauty of West Sonoma, which seems to enjoy a more comfortable pace than might be enjoyed in other parts of the bustling county of Sonoma. Set in Sebastopol's agriculture-rich country environment, guests at Holiday Inn Express are close to everything - the spectacular beaches, the thundering surf, all manner of recreational pursuits, and the famed Russian River Valley wine country. But there is more to Sebastopol. It is also a thriving art community. This interest in art is fostered at Holiday Inn Express by quarterly shows and sales of the works of local artists in the lobby, breakfast room and guest rooms. Health and business are also a consideration of the friendly lodging center, with an outdoor pool and spa, fitness room, in-room refrigerator, coffee maker, iron and ironing board and state of the art phone system with T1 lines, data port and voice mail. These amenities, plus a delightful complimentary Continental breakfast help explain why Holiday Inn Express was honored as an Excellent Quality Performer Hotel, and has earned three diamonds from the AAA.

*Holiday Inn Express Hotel & Suites, 1101 Gravenstein Highway South, Sebastopol, CA 95472. Telephone: 707-829-6677. Toll-free reservations: 800-465-4329. FAX: 707-829-2618. E-mail: holidayinn@lokhotels.com. Website: www.lokhotels.com. 82 rooms and meeting space for groups up to 45. Rates: $89.00 - $179.00.*

## THE HONOR MANSION

Local lore is filled with tales of extraordinary derring-do and unbelievable events of happenstance. Take for example the story of William "Squire" Butcher. During the days of '49, Butcher was transporting a load of pot bellied stoves to the mining camps, when the weight of the load collapsed his wagon, and the heavy stoves cracked the road to reveal a rich vein of gold beneath it.

He continued to prosper, and as his daughters reached school age, he wanted to build a home close to a fine Seventh Day Adventist school. He found his site on Grove St., in Healdsburg, and in 1883 constructed the beautiful Honor Mansion. Until 1994, when Steve and Cathi Fowler bought the mansion it had always been occupied by a family member. With respect for the history, the Fowlers renovated and redecorated the Mansion, turning it into an elegant bed and breakfast inn, with incredible attention to protecting the privacy of the guests. A full breakfast may be enjoyed in the dining room or on the deck beside the koi pond. Honor Mansion offers a full concierge service, lap pool and 1.5 acres of landscaped grounds. All the rooms have private baths, feather beds with down comforters, winter and summer bathrobes, luxurious imported toiletries, garment steamers, guest phones with dataports and voice mail and full turndown service, complete with mints on the pillow. The espresso/cappuccino machine is always ready and there is an endless supply of cookies and tea biscuits to go with your evening sherry.

*The Honor Mansion, 14891 Grove St., Healdsburg, CA 95448. Telephone 800-554-4667, FAX: 707-431-7173. E-mail: concierge@honormansion.com. Website: www.honormansion.com. Five guest rooms, 1 cottage and 3 suites. Rates: April 16 - November 14 - $180.00 -$330.00 per night; November 15 - April 15 - $190.00 - $350.00.*

## HOPE-BOSWORTH & HOPE-MERRILL HOUSE
### Bed and Breakfast
Facing each other across Geyserville Avenue are two grand examples of early 20th Century architecture, the Hope-Merrill House and Hope-Bosworth House. The Hope-Bosworth House, constructed in 1904 by pioneering settler George Bosworth is a charming Queen Anne, built from plans ordered from a "pattern book." Hope-Merrill is a striking 19th Century Eastlake Stick Style Victorian, originally the home of land developer

J. P. Merrill and his wife, Martha. Though occupied by many different families over the years, it was in 1980 that the two magnificent homes came back to life when Bob and Rosalie Hope began their transformation into a pair of bed and breakfast inns.

With great love, the Hopes sought out authentic wall papers and furnishings to restore the elegance of the two residences. Then they added their own touches of warmth and hospitality, created the singularly inviting Pick and Press Wine Making Event and soon were booked far into the future.

After Bob's death Rosalie was just about to put the inns on the market when Ron and Cosette Scheiber, visiting in the area with the object of finding a site for a bed and breakfast, heard about the possible sale. They met, and Rosalie, assured the Scheibers were going to lavish the same love and care as she had on the homes welcomed them as new owners.

Cosette and Ron have continued the traditions of marvelous home-cooked breakfasts, conversations about events and wineries in the area and the two-season "Crushing Good Time" winemaking festivities. All the rooms have queen-sized beds, private baths and all the amenitites a traveler relishes.

*Hope-Bosworth House & Hope-Merrill House, 21253 Geyserville Ave., Geyserville, CA 95441. Telephone: 800-825-4233, FAX: 707-857-4673. E-mail: moreinfo@hope-inns.com. Website: www.hope-inns.com. 12 rooms. Rates: $122.00 to $218.00.*

## HOTEL HEALDSBURG
Healdsburg's newest hotel is on the site of one of the oldest, the original Healdsburg Plaza Hotel, which was demolished more than 20 years ago. All that the weary traveler could ask for is here. The rooms and suites are elegantly furnished and have mini refrigerators, two-line portable phones, high speed Internet, CD players, oversized bathrooms with 6-ft. soaking tubs and walk-in showers and private balconies with views of the lively

Plaza below or the hotel's own grand gardens. For the health conscious. Hotel Healdsburg makes it utterly convenient to keep up with exercise regimes. There is the cardio-fitness room, a 60-ft. pool, and a complete spa with six treatment rooms offering a wide range of skin and body treatments, including facials, massage and manicure/pedicure. Lunch and dinner is served daily in the Dry Creek Kitchen, the creation of chef/author Charlie Palmer, winner of the prestigious "Ivy" award as restaurateur of distinction and the James Beard "Best Chef in New York," among many other accolades. Casual refreshments are offered at the Grappa Bar in the lobby and the Cafe International Newsstand, serving gelato, espresso and panini.

*Hotel Healdsburg, 25 Matheson St., Healdsburg, CA 95448. Telephone: 707-431-2800, FAX: 707-431-0414. E-mail: frontdesk@hotelhealdsburg.com. Website: hotelhealdsburg.com. There are 55 rooms, including six suites. Rates $205.00 - $450.00 Reservations must be guaranteed with a credit card. Charlie Palmer's Dry Creek Kitchen is open for lunch daily, 11:30AM - 3:30PM, and dinner, 5:00PM - 10:00PM. There is seating for 70 inside, and 20 in the country garden patio.*

## HOTEL LA ROSE

One of the prettiest buildings in Santa Rosa's historic Railroad Square is Hotel La Rose, which is listed with the Historical Hotels of America. It was built in 1907 by Italian stone masons and retains much of the charm and strength of the craggy stone exterior. Modernization has kept the comfort level high and despite extensive remodeling and the addition of a Carriage House across the street, Hotel La Rose retains the hospitality and appointments of a small European-style hotel, complete with an excellent restaurant, Josef's, which is open to the public as well as guests and serving dinner from 5:30PM - 9:00PM.

*Hotel La Rose, 308 Wilson St., Santa Rosa, CA 95401. Telephone: 707-579-3200, FAX: 707-579-3247. E-mail: concierge@hotellarose.com. Website: www.hotellarose.com. 49 rooms with rates from $165.00 - $199.00.*

## HUCKLEBERRY SPRINGS

Huckleberry Springs Country Inn and Spa is about as close as you can come to having your own secluded and private cabin on a mountaintop with an expansive view of the verdant Russian River Valley. Each of the four charming cottages is architecturally different, tucked into the 56-acre resort in comfortable harmony with its surroundings. Each cottage has a VCR, CD and cassette players, small refrigerator, coffee maker, hair dryer and flashlight. Three have queen beds, one has a king, and three have wood-burning stoves. All have skylights over the bed, and private bathrooms with showers. Guest amenities include a swimming pool, outdoor Jacuzzi space in a landscaped gazebo and a private massage cottage with spa therapies. Breakfast each morning is served in the Lodge, and although you may have to leave your own pet at home, there are two cats and two bouncy terriers "on staff" who will welcome your pats and strokes.

*Huckleberry Springs Country Inn & Spa, 8105 Old Beedle Rd., Monte Rio, CA 95462. Telephone: 707-865-2683 or 800-822-2683. E-mail: mail@huckleberrysprings.com. Website: www.huckleberrysprings.com. Because of fire danger, the complete property is non-smoking. Rates range from $145.00 (single) and $175.00 double occupancy, to $225.00 (triple). A four course dinner is served Wednesday and Saturday evenings at $35.00 per person, with reservations.*

## INN AT THE TIDES RESORT AND CONFERENCE CENTER

If you have seen the Hitchcock thriller, "The Birds," then you have seen the Inn at the Tides, where many of the exciting scenes were filmed. But no film could do justice to the magnificence and beauty of the setting of the Inn on a hillside with sweeping views of the Pacific Ocean to the far horizon. Guest rooms feature bay and harbor views, in-room coffeemakers, hair dryers, refrigerators, plush terry robes, morning newspapers and irons/ironing boards. Many of the rooms have cozy fireplaces, and others are furnished with king sized beds. A continental breakfast is complimentary and room service is available for breakfast, dinner or cocktails. There are two restaurants: The Bay View Restaurant and Lounge, open for dinner Wednesday through Sunday and Tides Wharf & Restaurant, serving breakfast, lunch and dinner with full bar service every day. For total relaxation, The Inn at the Tides provides a heated swimming pool, spa, sauna, exercise facilities and can schedule a soothing massage at your best time, in the privacy of your own accommodations.

*The Inn at the Tides, 800 Highway One, Bodega Bay, CA 94923. Telephone: 800-541-7788, FAX: 707-875-2669. E-mail: iatt@monitor.net. Website: www.innatthetides.com or www.bodegabayinfo.com. 86 guest rooms, two restaurants. Rates: June16-November 14 from $189.00-299.00. November 15-June 15 from $159.00-269.00.*

## JENNER INN & COTTAGES

Families and romantic couples who vacation together do not often find such a marvelous choice of accommodations as is offered at Jenner Inn & Cottages. Visitors may select a room, a cottage, or one of the two bedroom homes on the historic property. One cottage, called the Tree House, is a reconstructed and renovated cabin where transient mill workers stayed during the big timber cutting years. Another, believed to be the home of the former mill manager, is known as Mill Cottage. And the largest quarters, Jenner House, has rooms named for each of the Jenner family members. Water front rooms have panoramic views of the Russian River estuary and Pacific Ocean. All the rooms have sun decks, and many have spas. Yoga classes are offered. Guests are treated to a country breakfast each morning in the Jenner Inn Lodge dining room and for relaxing after the day's adventures there is the Fireside Lounge and wine bar.

*Jenner Inn and Cottages, 10400 Coast Highway 1, Jenner, CA 95450. Telephone: 707-865-2377 or 800-732-2377. FAX: 707-865-0829. Website: www.jennerinn.com. Accommodation rates range from $98.00 per night to $378 for an elegant cliffside home. November through March, Sunday through Thursday 15% discount, exclusive of holidays.*

## MAC ARTHUR PLACE

It is possible that Sonoma County has more than its share of noble turn-of-the-century mansions, beautifully preserved and, in most cases, living a second charmed life. Think for a moment of the Burris-Good estate. Five generations of the Burris family occupied the property, which was known for gracious hospitality and gala events. The next owners, the Good family, enhanced the gardens and continued the pattern of gracious living. Then, in 1997, the mansion and grounds were restored and turned into MacArthur Place, a 35-room country inn. Six new cottages were added to the original manor house and barn, along with a full-service

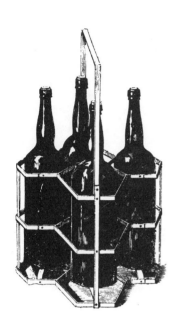

spa and Saddles Steakhouse. Another expansion in 2000 added 29 new suites, a library and courtyard. Each room in this historic country estate is individually designed and perfectly appointed. Walking the grounds is like being in a small Victorian village, and for the junket into town, there are bicycles just waiting for a foot on the pedal. (See also "Dining")

*MacArthur Place Inn & Spa, 29 E. MacArthur St., Sonoma CA 95476. Telephone: 707-938-2929, FAX: 707-933-9833. E-mail: info@macarthurplace.com. Website: www.macarthurplace.com. 64 rooms and suites, with rates that range from $269.00 to $750.00. Complimentary Continental breakfast, evening wine and cheese reception and a full-service spa and fully equipped fitness center, outdoor pool and whirlpool.*

## MADRONA MANOR, WINE COUNTRY INN & RESTAURANT

John Alexander Paxton was an extremely wealthy man, who knew exactly what he wanted. When he bought a 240-acre site for his home, he hired the finest architects and builders who created for him Madrona Knoll Rancho, the grandest showplace mansion that anyone had seen in decades. Though the family was beset by tragedy, the magnificent home lived on welcoming other families until 1981 when it was purchased to be transformed into a majestic bed and breakfast inn with an outstanding restaurant. There are five historic structures on the property – The Mansion, Carriage House and Schoolhouse Suites, Meadow Wood and Garden Cottage. The estate is surrounded by eight acres of manicured lawns, terraced flower and vegetable gardens and wooded areas. Antique furnishings, many original to the property, add to the atmosphere of elegance. In the kitchen of the four-star restaurant, chef Jesse Mallgren delights in preparing spectacular dinners in the romantic dining rooms and terrace. A generous breakfast buffet is included with your stay.

*Madrona Manor, Wine Country Inn & Restaurant, 1001 Westside Rd., Healdsburg, CA 95448. Telephone: 800-258-4003, FAX: 707-433-0703. E-mail: madronamanor@aol.com. Website: www.madronamanor.com. 17 rooms, five suites with private baths. Heated pool open May through October. Data port for web connection in each room. Rates: $175.00 - $455.00.*

## MELITTA STATION INN

The Melitta Station first welcomed guests in the late 1800s, and later became a depot for the Southern Pacific Railroad. As freight and transportation modes changed, Melitta Station found still another life as an inn. This turn of the century railroad station was caringly and lovingly restored into a five room (one suite) bed and breakfast and family home. All of the rooms are furnished with antiques and country collectibles, and each has a private bath. Guests enjoy an ample breakfast on the inn's balcony under the graceful boughs of the surrounding pepperwood trees. In the evening, the sideboard is set with wine and other refreshments, and a glass of sherry to cap the day.

*Melitta Station Inn, 5850 Melitta Rd., Santa Rosa, CA 95409. Telephone: 707-538-7712 or 800-504-3099. FAX: 707-538-7565. E-mail: melittasta@aol.com. Website: www.melittastationinn.com. Rates range from $100.00 to $175.00. Advance reservations are required.*

## MIDNIGHT SUN INN

Even though the charming building in which the Midnight Sun Inn is set was built after the earthquake of 1906, the rooms are contemporary and comfortable. There is air conditioning, and superbly cozy queen beds. All have private baths - two have Jacuzzi tubs. If it's peace and quiet you seek, this is the spot, just five blocks from the Healdsburg Plaza, but pleasantly situated in a tranquil residential area. Owners Monte Vinson and Christine Vinson offer concierge service, helpful advice and attention to every detail.

*Midnight Sun Inn, 428 Haydon St., Healdsburg, CA 95448. Telephone: 707-433-1718. FAX: 707-395-0244. E-mail: mvinson@sonic.net. Website: www.midnight-sun.com. Peak season rates are $145.00 - $165.00.*

## NORTHWOOD LODGE & RESORT

Whether your get-away plans are based around a fun-filled, exhilarating two-weeks with pay vacation, or a simple weekend escape, there's a great place to do that relaxing. It's called Northwood Lodge & Resort and the accommodations in the Lodge can be as simple or grand as you prefer. Just looking for a place to lay your head after exploring the coast and the river all day? Check into a room with a double, queen or king-sized

bed. If there are more than two in your party, select the more deluxe quarters, with two beds, a/c, microwave and refrigerator. Or, for the ultimate in privacy and contentment, nestle into one of the cottages under the redwoods. It's homelike, but so much better, with a large deck, living room with fireplace, full kitchen, dining area, wet bar and color cable TV. Guests may even enjoy use of outdoor barbecue facilities and, of course, there are the resort's pool, golf course and restaurant, all in an idyllic setting that you'll hate to leave to return to the realities of life. Weekday golf packages are available.

*Northwood Lodge & Resort, 19455 Highway 116, Monte Rio, CA 95462. Telephone: 707-865-1655. FAX: 707-865-1657. E-mail: info@northwood-lodge.com. Website: www.northwood-lodge.com. All units are non-smoking. Pool is open from 9:00 a m - 9:00 p m. Minimum two-night stay on weekends, three nights on holidays. Rates range from $69.00 - $285.00.*

## QUALITY INN, PETALUMA

At the northern edge of Petaluma, one of the oldest cities in California, founded in 1858, stands the distinctive Cape Cod style building that is the Quality Inn, winner of the Choice Hotels Gold Award, and rated three diamonds by the AAA. Built in 1985, located conveniently near Historic Downtown Petaluma, and refurbished in 2002, the 110-room Quality Inn serves as the travelers' comfortable and convenient hub to both the leisure of the wine country and the bustle of the area's burgeoning industry. To meet its aim of providing its guests with a friendly stay in a family-oriented atmosphere, Quality Inn offers an outdoor pool and spa, dry heat sauna, fitness room, in-room refrigerator and coffee maker, guest coin laundry, modem-friendly state of the art phone system, voice mail and one of the county's most delicious complimentary Continental breakfasts.

*Quality Inn, Petaluma, 5100 Montero Way, Petaluma, CA 94954. Telephone: 707-664-1155; toll-free reservations: 800-228-5151. Fax 707-664-8566. E-mail: qualityinns@lokhotels.com. Website: www.lokhotels.com. 110 rooms with rates from $89.00 - $179.00.*

## RAFORD HOUSE BED AND BREAKFAST INN

When Raford W. Peterson built his summer home, in the 1880s, the view from his windows was of tall trellised vines of hops. Fortunately, things have changed considerably in the intervening hundred or so years and now guests at Raford House, a Sonoma County Historical Landmark, are surrounded by towering palm trees, old-fashioned flower gardens and luxuriant vineyards. There are six guest rooms on two floors. One of the most spectacular is the Blue Room, on the second floor, which was the parlor in the original home. On the first floor is the Bridal Room, the largest of the guest accommodations. The Bridal Room has an outside entrance through French doors with a private covered porch, a wood-burning fireplace and a dream-inspiring library.

*Raford House Bed & Breakfast, 10630 Wohler Rd., Healdsburg, CA 95448. Telephone: 800-887-9503, or 707-887-9573. FAX: 707-887-9597. Website: www.rafordhouse.com. Rates range from $130.00 to $195.00. There is a two-night minimum stay requirement on weekend reservations, April through November, holiday and special event weekends. Smoking is permitted in the veranda and garden areas only.*

## RIDENHOUR RANCH HOUSE INN

It's one thing to dream of owning and operating a charming bed and breakfast, but the reality struck home full force for Chris Bell and Meilani Naranjo, when they became the proud owners of Ridenhour Ranch House, and had 12 guests to prepare breakfast for on their first day. They still love the inn, a handsome ranch house constructed in 1906 by Louis Ridenhour, on his 940 acre ranch that stretched out on both sides of the Russian River. There are eight rooms, all with private baths and either queen or king-sized beds. Amenities include fluffy terry robes, and a guest kitchen stocked with complimentary water, soft drinks, juices, port and sherry. Relaxation is supreme at the inn, helped along by an outdoor redwood hot tub. Mornings start with a full breakfast, and each afternoon, as a special treat, home-baked cookies emerge from the oven. If you're really seeking to get away from it all, two of the cozy rooms are TV-free!

*Ridenhour Ranch House Inn, 12850 River Rd., Guerneville, CA 95446. Telephone: 707-887-1033 or toll-free, 888-877-4466. FAX: 707-869-2967. E-mail: ridenhourinn@earthlink.net. Website: www.ridenhourranchhouseinn.com. Smoking permitted in outdoor patio areas, only. Rates: $105.00 - $185.00.*

## RIO INN

This spot beside the Russian River has been a refreshing stop for weary travelers since the turn of the century, and innkeeper Dawson Church promises to make each guest's stay a memorable and welcome respite from the cares and drudgery of the daily rat race. The Rio Inn features traditional Tudor architecture, with old world grace and charm. Each room is charmingly furnished with antiques, heirlooms and original art, with a selection of classic and contemporary reading materials for those loafing moments, and walking trails beside the River and under the redwoods, for casual strolling. Rio Inn also welcomes conferences, parties and retreats, and its Druid's Circle redwood grove, paneled Guild Hall and the intimate Victoria Parlor have become famous as attractive settings for weddings, outdoors or in. There is a spa and a workout room, and each day begins with a home-cooked breakfast.

*Rio Inn, 4444 Wood Rd., Guerneville, CA 95446. Telephone: 707-869-4444. Website: www.rioinn.com. Rates: $89.00 - $149.00; Cardiff House, $325.00, Sherwood Cottage, $275.00.*

## RIVER VILLAGE RESORT & SPA

No newcomers to the scene, innkeepers Donna and Gary Klauenburch have lived on a ranch above Armstrong Woods State Park (Guerneville) for more than 20 years. After spending a year renovating and hand crafting 20 cottages that fit into the wooded landscape naturally and comfortably, the Klauenburchs completed the picture by adding a complete spa, offering signature spa services and using the highest quality locally made organic herbal spa products. There is a pool with a large outdoor hydrotherapy spa, private massage rooms with soaking tubs and aromatherapy. All the cottages feature private bathrooms and kitchenettes with microwaves and refrigerators. A stroll through the beautifully landscaped gardens with its unusual collection of native plants and herbs is an enjoyable learning experience. A Continental breakfast is offered each morning beside the pool. Lounging is encouraged on large private decks and a forested path leads through the redwoods behind the resort.

*River Village Resort and Spa, 14880 River Rd., Guerneville, CA 95446. Telephone: 707-869-8139 or 800-529-3376, FAX: 707-869-3096. E-mail: info@rivervillageresort.com. Website: www.rivervillageresort.com. 17 rooms and three apartments at rates ranging from $90.00 - $195.00. Complete spa services. Designated smoking areas.*

## RIVERLANE RESORT

When you want to get away from it all to spend some time dreaming under the redwoods, or sitting on a beach beside the Russian River, but you also want the freedom to fix what you really want to eat, whenever you want to eat it, the place to call for a reservation is Riverlane Resort in Guerneville. At Riverlane there are 13 housekeeping cabins, with fully equipped kitchens, decks with picnic tables, and barbecues, to accommodate one to eight people. Here's a word to the wise: mid-week reservations are easier to make, particularly for those spring and autumn get-aways, and even in a storm, a stay at Riverlane can be a rejuvenating experience, as you watch nature's handiwork in action.

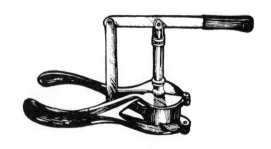

To keep your larder stocked, there is a 24-hour supermarket one block away, and if you get tired of your own cooking, there are 15 restaurants within easy walking distance. Fish or swim at the river beach or rent a kayak, canoe, or bicycle and go exploring.

*Riverlane Resort, 16320 First St., corner of Church St., Guerneville, CA 95446. Telephone: 707-869-2323 or 800-201-2324. FAX: 707-869-1954. E-mail: rivlares@sonic.net. Website: www.riverlaneresort.com. Daily rates range from $65.00 - $120.00, weekly, from $350.00 - $585.00. All rates are 20% less, mid-October – mid-April, when the pool is closed.*

## SEA RANCH LODGE

Unique is a very over-worked word in the travel business, but there is one Sonoma County destination for which the word unique would seem to be made. The Sea Ranch Lodge, on Highway One just south of Gualala, is part of the environmentally and ecologically planned community of The Sea Ranch. Like all the homes and buildings on the ten-mile property, the architecture of the Lodge echoes the slope of the hills and the natural weathering of the woods used in its construction makes it fit almost invisibly into the surrounding terrain. Yet the lodge offers, inside its rustic walls, all the modern comforts and amenities of the glitziest hotel. The 20 ocean view guest rooms all have plush down comforters, individual climate control and two-line phones with data ports. The earth and sea tones of the decor are accented with works by local artists. Gourmets come from as far away as San Francisco, 110 miles south, to dine on the fine Coastal Cuisine prepared by Executive Chef Jeffrey Longenecker at the Restaurant in the Lodge. For the outdoor enthusiast there are meadow and bluff-top trails, an off-road bicycle path and the challenging 18-hole golf links designed by Robert Muir Graves. Weddings, receptions and business meetings are easily and expertly arranged by the experienced Sea Ranch Lodge staff. (See also Dining).

*Sea Ranch Lodge, 60 Sea Walk Drive, The Sea Ranch, CA 95497. Telephone: 707-785-2371. Toll-free for reservations: 800-732-7262. FAX: 707-785-2917. Website: www.searanchlodge.com. 20 rooms, post office, gift shop, cocktail lounge, restaurant. Two meeting rooms and on-site assistance for planning weddings and/or retreats Rates: $205.00 - $395.00.*

## SEBASTOPOL INN

Taking a cue from its location in the historic Gravenstein Railroad Station, Sebastopol Inn reflects the architectural style of early 19th Century train depots, with vertical board and batten siding, verdigris copper roof and verandah porches set with courting swings and glider love seats. A garden courtyard is made musical with fountains, invitingly graced with arbors and swings and on-property is a luxurious heated pool and New Dawn Day spa. The interior is simple and understated, but replete with all the comforts the traveler expects. The 31 rooms and suites have queen or king beds, private baths, TV, phones and coffee-makers. Some rooms have fireplaces, Jacuzzi tubs, microwaves and refrigerators. The Balcony rooms look out on a wetland preserve, while the Courtyard rooms face the gardens. The New Dawn Day Spa offers a variety of massage, spa and facial skin care, and waxing treatments. Sebastopol's fascinating town center is just steps away, and walking trails lead through the beauty of the wetlands.

*Sebastopol Inn, 6751 Sebastopol Ave., Sebastopol, CA 95472. Telephone: 707-829-2500. FAX: 707-823-1535. Website: www.sebastopolinn.com. 31 rooms and suites at rates from $112.00 - $162.00. The inn is a non-smoking facility.*

## SHERATON PETALUMA HOTEL

One of Sonoma County's newest premium hotels is the Sheraton Petaluma perched on the Petaluma Marina adjacent to 300 acres of protected wetlands. The architectural design of the four-story building follows the clean, fresh lines of the existing Marina building to give guests a feeling of comfortable elegance at the gateway to the North Coast Wine Country. With 183 guest rooms and nearly 10,000 sq. ft. of flexible meeting space, Sheraton Petaluma can host a range of conferences and meetings with different space requirements from the spacious 4300 sq. ft. grand ballroom to the most intimate of conference rooms. There is a full range of AV equipment and world-class catering and banquet service. All rooms include laptop-sized safes and refrigerators. One bi-level presidential suite features a home theater surround-sound system and 60" TV. Each guest room has state-of-the-art phone and high-speed data systems. For dining the hotel's signature restaurant, Jellyfish, has an elegant lounge, full service cocktail bar, patio seating and raw bar. The fitness center is equipped with saunas with direct access to the outdoor swimming pool and spa.

*Sheraton Petaluma Hotel, 745 Baywood Drive, Petaluma, CA 94954. Telephone: 707-283-2888, 800-325-3535. FAX: 707-283-2828. Website: www.sheratonpetaluma.com. 183 rooms: traditional rooms $140.00-250.00, Deluxe rooms, Club Level rooms and Suites, $250.00-500.00 per night.*

## SONOMA CHALET BED & BREAKFAST

Set on three bucolic acres in the storied Valley of the Moon, Sonoma Chalet is surrounded by the beauty and history of Sonoma's colorful past. The Swiss-style farmhouse and country cottages provide guests with a choice of individually decorated rooms filled with antiques, quilts and collectibles. There is a choice of a fireplace or wood stove, and each room has a balcony or deck for those lazy moments when the only proper activity seems to be to sit back and enjoy the scenery. For storybook perfection, many guests choose "Sara's Cottage." Across a wooden footbridge the gem of a cottage looks as if it were the centerpiece of a fairy tale, with a cozy sleeping area and loft, a spacious private bath with claw-foot tub and a library of books you've always meant to read when you had time.. A Continental breakfast each morning is served in the colorful kitchen of the farmhouse or on the deck overlooking the ranch grounds.

*Sonoma Chalet Bed & Breakfast, 18935 Fifth St. West, Sonoma, CA 95476. Telephone: 707-938-3129. Website: www.sonomachalet.com. Four rooms, three cottages, at rates from $110.00 - $225.00. Smoking is permitted only in the outside garden and deck areas.*

## SONOMA COAST VILLA

Where cattle once grazed 100 or so years ago above the rugged Sonoma County coastline, an elegant country inn has risen, looking for all the world like a bit of Tuscany transplanted to California's west coast. The inn features 18 Mediterranean influenced rooms, personally decorated with their own distinctive style by Susan Griffin, the inn's co-owner. Features include wood-burning fireplaces, Jacuzzi tubs, slate floors and exposed wooden beams. When the guest checks into his/her room, a fruit basket, snacks, a bottle of local wine, a stock of sodas and beer, freshly ground coffee and an assortment of teas awaits. Often guests choose to begin the day with a fragrant aromatherapy massage at the Courtyard Spa, or perhaps a massage or mud wrap. A dip in the pool is always welcome, and down the path, in the Carriage House, one can play ping pong, shoot pool or engage in a challenging board game. The Tower Library is a perfect spot for birdwatchers to add to their life lists. Co-owner Cyrus Griffin is the genius with whisk and beater, whipping up extraordinary country breakfasts each morning, and dinner buffets Friday and Saturday evenings for guests who don't want to leave the Villa.

*Sonoma Coast Villa Inn & Spa, 16702 Coast Highway One, Bodega, CA 94922. Telephone: 707-876-9818 or toll free 888-404-2255, FAX: 707-876-9856. E-mail: reservations@scvilla.com. Website: www.scvilla.com. 16 rooms currently, 18 rooms in 2002. Spa and pool. Rates: $225.00 - $325.00. Spa reservations suggested one week prior to arrival.*

## THE SONOMA HOTEL

When Henry Wehl built the building which today is The Sonoma Hotel, in 1880, the ground floor contained a dry goods store and a butcher shop. The second floor resounded to the jollity of a community/social hall. In the 1920s the Sebastiani family transformed the edifice into a charming inn and renamed it "The Plaza Hotel." Then, along came innkeepers Tim Farfan and Craig Miller who remodeled the hotel in 1999, adding private baths, TV, telephones, air-conditioning and the tasteful decor of antiques and French country furniture. Right on the historic Sonoma City Plaza, The Sonoma Hotel is not just charming and comfortable, but convenient to historical sites, restaurants, shops, and some of the most distinguished wineries in the county. A Continental breakfast is served each morning, and there is complimentary wine tasting to welcome travelers home after a day of exploration. The Sonoma Hotel is a non-smoking hotel. Access to second floor is by stairs only.

*The Sonoma Hotel, 110 West Spain St., Sonoma, CA 95476. Telephone: 707-996-2996 or 800-468-6016, FAX: 707-996-7014. E-mail: sonomahotel@aol.com. Website: www.sonomahotel.com. 16 rooms, including one petite suite. Rates: $145.00 - $245.00.*

## SONOMA MISSION INN & SPA

Since the days when the Miwok Indians lived in the Sonoma Valley, the therapeutic and beneficial properties of the local hot springs have been recognized. Early settlers, in the mid-1800s, constructed bath houses over the springs and soon people were flocking to the primitive resorts to enjoy the hot vapors. Later residents dug wells and captured the hot mineral springs in tubs, which brought more visitors. By the turn of the century, a hotel had been constructed, along with some cottages, tent houses, a bathhouse, a large swimming pool and a bottling works. This grandiose settlement was destroyed by fire in 1923 and a new larger hotel was built on the site and given the new name Sonoma Mission Inn. Though the name is the same, the Sonoma Mission Inn of today, with its 228 rooms, European-style spa and two restaurants is far grander, more comfortable and attentive to its guests' needs than the early resort owners could ever have dreamed of. Guests at the inn are welcomed with a bottle of wine and find in their rooms soft, plush terry cloth robes, Sonoma Mission Inn signature Apricot & Cream bath amenities and two line telephones with dataports. Guests are treated to a Continental breakfast each morning, an evening wine tasting reception and can participate in planned hikes or fitness classes in the fitness center.

*Sonoma Mission Inn & Spa, 18140 Sonoma Hwy. (Highway 12), Sonoma, CA 95476. Telephone: 707-938-9000, FAX: 707-938-4250. E-mail: smi@smispa.com. Website: www.sonomamissioninn.com. 228 rooms at rates from $279.00 - $1200.00. Two restaurants: The Restaurant at the Sonoma Mission Inn & Spa, open daily 6:00PM - 10:00PM. Big 3 Diner, open daily, 7:00AM - 9:30PM.*

## THISTLE DEW INN

There is an interesting story about how the Thistle Dew Inn came to be. The house on the rear of the property was built in 1869 and was originally on the front of the lot. In 1980 the house was moved back and a second house, built in 1905 and resting a few blocks away, was moved onto the land. In its transformation into an inn, the homes were furnished with museum quality Arts and Crafts furniture. The inn's second owners added additional baths and a hot tub and began to soften the rather Spartan colors and decor of the rooms. Then came Larry and Norma Barnett, in 1990, who embarked on a complete remodel, turning the small rooms into six deluxe accommodations with private entrances and decks. Larry also created a cactus garden with his collection of 300 cacti and succulents and created a number of cozy garden spots with colorful roses and perennials and a number of bubbling fountains. The days at Thistle Dew Inn begin with a gourmet breakfast served in the inn's dining room and conclude in the afternoon with complimentary hors d'oeuvres to bring the day to a pleasant conclusion.

*Thistle Dew Inn, 171 West Spain St., Sonoma, CA 95476. Telephone: 800-382-7895 or 707-938-2909. Website: www.thistledew.com. Six rooms at rates from $135.00-210.00; $150.00-250.00 weekends. Smoking permitted on outdoor decks and patios. Complimentary use of bicycles.*

## VILLA MESSINA

Anyone crazy about stunning views is going to find Villa Messina the ideal spot to spend a few days or more. The elegant villa, constructed atop an abandoned reservoir which once served historic Simi winery, offers a 360-degree view which overlooks the famous Dry Creek and Alexander Valleys and stretches to Geyser Peak on the west - often crowned with puffy steam clouds from the geysers. Each of the five beautifully appointed rooms has a private bath, TV, VCR, a private phone and either a queen or king-sized bed. The word leisure takes on a new meaning as guests relax on the wrap-around deck with vineyard views in all directions. Each afternoon the deck is made even jollier with a wine and cheese interval, as the lap pool glistens invitingly just a step or two away. For those who miss their pets left at home, there's a great family of four-footed friends to visit with: Zorba and Cancun, the llamas and the house favorites, the West Highland Terriers.

*Villa Messina, 316 Burgundy Rd., Healdsburg, CA 95448. Telephone: 707-433-6655, FAX: 707-433-4515. Website: www.villamessina.com. Five rooms with rates from $200.00 - $350.00.*

TRAVEL NOTES: _____

## VINTNERS INN

Vintners Inn and John Ash & Co. restaurant, together form one of Sonoma County's favorite spots for lodging and dining. Located just to the northwest of Santa Rosa, the county seat of Sonoma County, this 90-acre resort hotel property offers European style and charm unrivaled in the county. Its 44 guest rooms are artfully housed in three separate buildings, grouped around a central courtyard with a magnificent three-tiered custom-made fountain. Spacious grounds filled with the vibrant color of flowers are in turn surrounded by lush rows of vines as far as the eye can see. This secluded getaway is perfect for both the leisure and business traveler. In addition to the unabashed luxury of guest rooms and suites, Vintners Inn offers business facilities that can be customized for a wide variety of purposes. See also Dining.

*Vintners Inn, 4350 Barnes Rd., Santa Rd., CA 95403.*
*Telephone: 707-575-7350.*
*Website: www.vintnersinn.com. 44 rooms in*
*Mediterranean-style luxury. For rates and information,*
*call 800-421-2584, or visit the website.*

TRAVEL NOTES: _____
_____
_____
_____
_____
_____
_____
_____

Events

t is absolutely true that no matter what time of year a traveler visits Sonoma County there is certain to be some special and entertaining event going on. Many of these naturally involve food and wine - there are spaghetti feeds, pancake breakfasts, crab fests and all manner of fiestas that celebrate the bounty of the county's abundance of fruit, produce, fish and dairy products, along with displays of arts and crafts. The Farmers' Markets and Farm Trails salute each crop as its season dawns, and those looking for culture will find musical events in abundance, art walks and gallery shows and a dozen or so theatrical venues. Because the county is blessed with this plenty, our listing can only accommodate the major, dependably scheduled events. Local newspapers, the county website and chambers of commerce can fill in the missing links. Dates subject to change. All information was correct on date of publication.

## JANUARY

Third weekend: Winter Wineland, tasting of food and wine, entertainment and education at the 50+ wineries along the Russian River Wine Road. 800-723-6336.

Fourth Saturday: Old Time Fiddle Contest. Contestants vie for prizes, each playing a waltz and a hoedown. Citrus Fairgrounds, Cloverdale. 707-894-2067

## FEBRUARY

President's Holiday Weekend: California North Coast Wine Tasting. Tasting of 600 prize-winning wines from North Coast Wine competition. Citrus Fairgrounds, Cloverdale. 707-894-3992

Mid-February: Romancing the Vine. Wine and food extravaganza. Sonoma County Museum. 707-579-1500.

## MARCH

First Weekend: Barrel Tasting. Russian River Wine Road wineries and growers offer tastes of wines still in formative stage, along with food, vineyard tours, music, fun and sale of wine futures. 800-723-6336.

Mid-March Fourth Saturday: Symphony of Food and Wine. Food, wine tasting and Music by Santa Rosa Symphony Youth Orchestra. 80 wineries and restaurants participating. Santa Rosa Veterans Memorial Building. 707-546-8742.

Last weekend in March, first of April: Sonoma Valley Film Festival. 707-258-5929.

## APRIL

Early April: Wine Country Cycling Classic. Saturday event: 100-mile competition, traveling west Sonoma countryside. Sunday, 90-minute speed race through downtown Santa Rosa, bike festival. 707-579-0413.

Mid-April: April in Carneros. Wineries in Carneros Appellation hold open house for tasting and entertainment. 800-654-9463.

Mid-April: Bodega Bay Fisherman's Festival. Blessing of the Fleet, boat parade, bathtub race, food, wine, arts and crafts. Most events at Westside Park, Bodega Bay. 707-875-3422.

Third Saturday: Pick of the Vine. Outstanding food and wine pairings. Friedman Center, Santa Rosa. 707-526-4108.

Last Saturday: Butter and Egg Days; Parade, floats, horses, booths, entertainment. Downtown Petaluma. 707-762-9348.

Simultaneous with above: Opening Day of the Petaluma River. Decorated boats and costumed crews.

Last Sunday: Outdoor Antique Fair with 200 vendors, in Historic Downtown Petaluma. 707-765-1155 Downtown River Harbor. 707-765-6750.

Last Weekend: Sebastopol Apple Blossom Festival. Downtown parade, food and wine pavilion, music, flower show, apple exhibits. Ives Park, Sebastopol. 707-823-3032.

Last Weekend: Passport to Dry Creek Valley. By advance reservation only. Special celebrations, tasting of rare wines, vineyard tours. Throughout Dry Creek Valley, west of Healdsburg. 707-433-3031.

## MAY

First Saturday: May Day Festival. May Pole, food booths, fire brigade water fight, music and entertainment. Geyser Peak Picnic Grounds, Geyserville. 707-857-3745.

First Sunday: Day under the Oaks. Annual open house and education fair at Santa Rosa Junior College. Demonstrations and Exhibits. 707-527-4266.

First Sunday: 4-H Chicken-Que. Chicken barbecue dinner, booths, livestock exhibits, games, community safety fair. Sonoma County Fairgrounds, Santa Rosa. 707-565-2681.

Second Saturday: Human Race. Annual walk/run through Santa Rosa's Howarth and Spring Lake parks. Fund-raiser for 400 charities. Optional: Mountain bike ride through Annadel State Park. 707-573-3399.

Second Saturday: Old Adobe Living History Day. A celebration of the 1840s with costumed volunteers demonstrating crafts and cooking of that era. Old Adobe, Petaluma. 707-762-4871.

Mid-May: Luther Burbank Rose Parade & Festival. Two hour parade with 100 performing units, floats, rose bloom competition, food, and music. Juilliard Park, Santa Rosa. 707-542-7673.

Mid-May: Healdsburg Future Farmer and 4-H Country Fair. Opens with Twilight Parade, Thursday evening. Livestock competition, auction, exhibits, ugly dog contest, chili contest. Recreation Park, Healdsburg. 707-431-7644.

Memorial Day Weekend: Outdoor Antique Fair in the city Plaza, Healdsburg. 707-433-4315.

## JUNE

First Weekend: Taste of the Valley. Alexander Valley wineries open for cave and cellar tours, barrel tasting, farmers markets. 888-289-4637.

First Sunday: 33rd Annual Sonoma Ox Roast. Old-fashioned picnic as experienced in pioneer days, preceded by 10K/2.2K walk Barbecue, music, arts and crafts. Historic Plaza, Sonoma. 707-938-4626.

First Weekend: Stumptown Daze Parade and Rodeo. Parade Saturday, rodeo Saturday and Sunday. Barbecue, crafts fair. Downtown Guerneville. 707-869-9000.

Second Weekend: Health and Harmony Festival. Environmental and health fair with 500 exhibits, music, dance, entertainment. Sonoma County Fair Grounds, Santa Rosa. 707-575-9355.

Mid-June: Cloverdale Heritage Days. 3K and 10K runs, wine tasting, music, entertainment, cow chip toss, old-time fashion show. City park and downtown Cloverdale. 707-894-4470.

Mid-June: Red & White Ball. Wine, hors d'oeuvres, dancing to live band. Historic Plaza, Sonoma. 707-996-3885.

Last Weekend: Festival of the Arts. Outdoor celebration of arts and crafts in town of Duncans Mills. 707-824-8404.

Late June: Sonoma County Hot Air Balloon Classic. Pancake breakfast, craft booths, displays, continuous entertainment. 50 hot air balloons taking flight. Near Shiloh Rd. and Highway 101, Windsor. 707-836-0777.

## JULY

Fourth of July Fireworks: Bodega Bay, Guerneville, Healdsburg, Petaluma, Rohnert Park, Sebastopol and Windsor.

Fourth of July Celebrations:
Kenwood - 3K and 10K races, food, music, World Pillow Fight Championship. Plaza Park, Kenwood. 707-833-2440.

Santa Rosa - Picnic on the lawn, food booths, music. Sonoma County Fairgrounds, Santa Rosa. 707-542-5803.

Sonoma - Parade, displays at Vallejo Home, State Historic Park, Sonoma. 707-938-4626.

Rohnert Park - Independence Day on the Green. Santa Rosa Symphony Pops Concert, lakeside on Sonoma State University campus, Rohnert Park. 707-546-8742.

Mid-July: Healdsburg Harvest Century Bicycle Tour, 60, 37 and 25 mile options. Routes wind through Alexander Valley, Dry Creek Valley, Russian River Valley. 707-433-6935.

Late July into August: Sonoma County Fair. Agriculture, livestock, food, arts, crafts, woodworking, plant exhibitions, horse races, carnival, Mexican Village. Sonoma County Fairgrounds, Santa Rosa. 707-545-4200.

Mid-June: Russian River Blues Festival. Outstanding blues festival with name performers. Johnson's Beach, Guerneville. 707-869-3940.

Mid-June: Sonoma-Marin Fair. Four days, open noon till midnight with carnival, car races, exhibits, entertainment. Sonoma-Marin Fairgrounds, Petaluma. 707-763-0931.

Mid-June: Juneteenth Celebration. Commemorating the day in 1865 when slaves in Texas learned of their freedom. Food, arts and crafts, music. South Wright Road, Santa Rosa. 707-546-6520.

## AUGUST

**First Weekend:** All Nations Big Time. Gathering of Native American artists. Craft show and sale, food, music, dancing. Adobe State Historical Park, Petaluma. 707-769-8920.

**Mid-August:** Wings Over Wine Country Air Show. Inspect, inside and out, historical aircraft at Pacific Coast Air Museum, Charles M. Schulz Sonoma County Airport, Santa Rosa. 707-575-7900.

**Mid-August:** Gravenstein Apple Fair. Saluting Sebastopol's famous apples with games, pies, food demonstrations. Ragle Ranch Park, Sebastopol. 707-571-8288.

**Mid-August:** Annual Santa Rosa Intertribal Powwow. American Indian cultural events with traditional dancing and drumming, arts and crafts, food, raffle. Sonoma County Fairgrounds, Santa Rosa. 707-869-8233.

**Late August:** Cotati Accordion Festival. Accordion workshops, craft and food booths, accordionists from around the world. Downtown Plaza, Cotati. 707-664-0444.

**Late August:** Seafood, Art & Wine Festival. Seafood sampling, wine and beer tasting, arts and crafts. Chanslor Ranch, Bodega Bay. 707-824-8404.

## SEPTEMBER

**Labor Day Weekend:** Sebastopol Cajun Fest. Cajun bands, jambalaya, gumbo, crawfish, red beans and rice. Laguna Park, Sebastopol. 707-823-1511.

**Labor Day Weekend:** Sonoma Valley Harvest Wine Auction. Fabulous wines from Sonoma Valley growers and wineries presented in light-hearted auction. Sonoma Mission Inn, Boyes Hot Springs. 707-938-1266.

**Second Weekend:** Heirloom Tomato Festival. Tomato art show, tomato contests, garden tours, food, wine, entertainment. Kendall-Jackson Wine Center, Windsor. 800-544-4413. Ext. 770.

**Second Weekend:** Cloverdale Street Celebration, Classic Car and Motorcycle Show. Car show to a 50s theme. Frog jumping contest. Downtown Cloverdale. 707-894-4470.

**Mid-September:** Glendi International Food Fair. Sample the cuisines of Greece, Russia, Bulgaria and more. Music, crafts and dancing. Mountain View Avenue, Santa Rosa. 707-584-9491.

**Mid-September:** Celtic Festival. Music, films, theater, crafts fair, all with a Celtic flavor. Downtown Sebastopol. 707-829-7067.

**Mid-September:** Something's Brewing. Beer tasting of brews from 25 breweries with foods from leading Sonoma County purveyors. Sonoma County Fairgrounds, Santa Rosa. 707-579-1500

**Late September:** Valley of the Moon Vintage Festival. A celebration of the grape harvest. Historic Plaza, Sonoma. 707-996-2109.

## OCTOBER

**First Weekend:** Sonoma County Harvest Fair. World championship grape stomp, tasting of medal-winning wines, food, arts and crafts, rodeo, kids exhibits, Christmas crafts, 10K race. Sonoma County Fairgrounds, Santa Rosa. 707-545-4203.

**Mid-October:** World Wristwrestling Championship. 500 entrants vying for the title. Semifinal and final competition at McNear's Mystic Theatre, Petaluma. 707-778-1430.

Late October: Fall Colors Festival and Antique car Show. Pancake breakfast, arts and crafts, car show, food booths, entertainment. Downtown Geyserville. 707-857-3745.

## NOVEMBER

First Weekend: A Food and Wine Affair. Members of Russian River Wine Road host food and wine celebrations at individual wineries. 800-723-6336.

Veterans Day Weekend: North Bay Veterans Day Parade. Marching bands, color guards, drill teams, antique military vehicles, veterans of five wars, and a fly-over by vintage aircraft. Parade starts at Walnut Park, Petaluma. 707-762-0591.

Mid-November: Santa Parade. Marching bands, costumed ïreindeer,î dancing snowflakes, Santa arrives on fire engine. Parade concludes with tree-lighting ceremony. Parade starts at Fourth and E streets, and ends at Courthouse Square, Santa Rosa. 707-528-6008.

Late November: Santa's River Boat Arrival & Antique Wagon Parade. Santa's arrival by boat at the Petaluma

Waterfront signals the start of a parade of antique wagons, decorated horse teams, and fairy tale characters on horseback. Procession winds through Historic downtown Petaluma. 707-769-0429.

## DECEMBER

First Weekend: Luther Burbank Home and Gardens Holiday Open House. Holiday gifts, food and crafts by local artisans. Burbank Home, Santa Rosa. 707-524-5445.

Early December: Russian River Heritage Christmas Celebration. Crafts fair, carriage rides, visits by Father Christmas, free trolley rides through town, tree lighting. Downtown Guerneville. 707-869-9000.

Pre-Christmas: Redwood Empire Sing-Along Messiah. Festival Chorus and all attendees. Luther Burbank Center for the Arts, Santa Rosa. 707-539-0495.

Adventures

ith the Pacific Ocean as its western border, the Russian River winding through its heart, 13 State Parks and 15 county parks within its boundaries and miles of country roads to explore, visitors who prefer to take their recreation out of doors have numberless opportunities to stretch their legs and necks checking out the glorious scenery of Sonoma County.

## OUTDOOR RECREATION AND ACTIVE SPORTS

### BICYCLING

Dave's Bike Sport and the Bike Peddler. Two locations in Santa Rosa. Sponsors of regularly scheduled recreational rides. Call 707-528-3283, or 707-571-2428.

Goodtime Bicycle Co., Sonoma. Bike rental, picnic rides and guided tours. Call 707-938-0453.

Rincon Cyclery, Santa Rosa. Bike, tandem, and car rack rental, custom and self-guided tours. Call 707-538-0868.

Sonoma Valley Cyclery, Sonoma. Bike rental. Call 707-935-3377.

Spoke Folk, Healdsburg. Bike rental, gear, maps. Call 707-433-7171.

### CANOES AND KAYAKS

California Rivers, Santa Rosa. Guided kayak tours on Russian River. Call 707-579-2209.

Burke's Russian River Canoe Trips, one mile north of Forestville, on banks of river. Open May to October. Self-guided 10-mile trip down Russian River to Guerneville. Shuttle service back to vehicle. Canoe, paddles, life jackets provided. No dogs, children under five or non-swimmers. Reservations necessary. Call 707-887-1222.

Trowbridge Canoe Trips, Healdsburg. Open spring to mid-October. Half day to five day self-guided trips along the Russian River. Family and group excursions. Call 707-433-7247.

### BOAT LAUNCHING

Lake Ralphine, Howarth Park, Santa Rosa. Paddle boats, canoes, rowboats, sailboats for rent. No motorized craft or boats longer than 20 feet. Call 707-543-4324.

Lake Sonoma Marina, off Skaggs Springs Road at Stewart's Point cutoff, Healdsburg. House boats, patio boats, jet skis, fishing boats for rent. Boat service and repair. Water ski school, picnic areas. Open all year; times vary. Call 707-433-2200.

Pacific Ocean, Doran, Westside Parks, Porto Bodega Marina ramp, all at Bodega Bay. Call 707-875-2354.

Petaluma River Marina, Petaluma. Fuel dock and 196 berths. Call 707-778-4489.

Russian River, downstream of Monte Rio Bridge on north bank, Monte Rio. Open June 1 to October 1. No phone number available. Other ramps at private campgrounds.

San Pablo Bay, Hudeman Slough below Sonoma Creek, Sonoma. Other free ramp locations nearby. No phone number available.

Spring Lake, Santa Rosa. Open all year. Hours vary. No gasoline-powered motors permitted. Call 707-539-8092.

## HIKING, HORSEBACK RIDING, AND MORE

Annadel State Park, Santa Rosa. Hiking, mountain biking, equestrian trails picnicking, fishing. Call 707-539-3911.

Armstrong Redwood State Reserve, Guerneville. Hiking and nature trails among tallest trees in Sonoma County. Bicycling, horseback riding, picnicking. Call 707-869-2015.

Armstrong Woods Pack Station, Guerneville. Guided trail rides and pack trips. Open daily. Call 707-887-2939.

Chanslor Guest Ranch, Bodega Bay. Guided trail rides on beach and ranch, barbecues. Call 707-875-2721.

Crane Creek Regional Park, Rohnert Park. Trails for hikers, cyclists, equestrians. Call 707-527-2041.

Doran Park, Bodega Bay. Vantage points for viewing whale migration, picnic areas, campgrounds, bird walk, horseback riding on the beach, fishing, clamming and surfing. Call 707-875-3540.

Helen Putnam Regional Park, Petaluma. Hiking, biking trails, picnic area, small playground. 707-565-2041.

Hood Mountain Regional Park, Kenwood. Hiking and equestrian trails. Open weekends and county holidays only. Call 707-565-2041.

Jack London State Historic Park, Glen Ellen. Hiking, nature trail, equestrian trail, self-guided history trail, author's grave, Wolf House ruins, museum. Open hours vary. Call 707-938-5216.

Kruse Rhododendron State Reserve, north of Jenner, next to Salt Point State Park. Hiking. Rhododendrons at height of bloom in May. Call 707-847-3221.

Lake Sonoma/Warm Springs Dam, Healdsburg. Visitor Center, fish hatchery, picnicking, horseback and hiking trails, boating, camping, fishing. Call 707-433-9483.

Maxwell Farms Regional Park, Sonoma. Nature trail, bicycle path, basketball court, tennis courts, volleyball, baseball, football and soccer fields, picnic area. Call 707-565-2041.

Ragle Ranch Regional Park, Sebastopol. Hiking and riding trails, bike path, soccer fields, volleyball, par course, picnic area. Call 707-565-2041.

Salt Point State Park, 20 miles north of Jenner on Highway 1. Hiking, bicycling, camping, picnicking, fishing, horseback riding, designated underwater area. Pygmy Forest. Call 707-847-3221.

Sonoma Cattle Co., Sonoma Valley. Individual and group rides at Jack London and Sugarloaf Ridge State Parks, with barbecues, lunch, winery tours, moonlight rides. Reservations necessary. Call 707-996-8566.

Sonoma State Beach, 13 miles of coastline from Russian Gulch to Bodega Head, including Bodega Dune and Wright's Beach campgrounds. Sites for hiking, bicycling, fishing, horseback riding, designated underwater areas. Call 707-865-2391.

Spring Lake Park, Santa Rosa. Hiking, equestrian trails, bike paths, visitor center, nature walks and displays, par course. In summer: swimming, boating, camping, picnicking. Call 707-565-2041.

Stillwater Cove Regional Park, 16 miles north of Jenner. Picnic areas, campgrounds, fishing, historic one-room schoolhouse. Call 707-847-3245.

Sugarloaf Ridge State Park, Kenwood. Hiking, horseback riding, camping, picnicking. Call 707-833-5712.

## GOLF

Virtually every city and community in Sonoma County has a golf course, from Cloverdale and Sea Ranch in the north and west, to Sonoma and Petaluma on the south. Hours and green fees vary. Please call for current information.

Adobe Creek Golf Club, Petaluma, 18 holes, par 72. Call 707-765-3000

Bennett Valley Golf Course, Santa Rosa. 18 holes, par 72. Call 707-528-3673.

Fairgrounds Golf Center and Driving Range, Santa Rosa. Nine holes, par 30. Call 707-527-0755.

Fountaingrove Country Club Golf Course, Santa Rosa. 18 holes, par 72. Call 707-579-4653.

Los Arroyos Golf Course, Sonoma. Nine holes, par 29. Call 707-938-8835.

Mountain Shadows Golf Resort, Rohnert Park. Two 18-hole courses, both par 72. Call 707-584-7766.

Northwood Golf Course, Monte Rio. Nine holes, par 36. Call 707-865-1116.

Oakmont Golf Club, Santa Rosa. Two 18-hole courses, par 72 and par 63. Call 707-539-0415.

Rooster Run Golf Course, Petaluma. 18 holes, par 72. Call 707-778-1211.

Sea Ranch Golf Links, Sea Ranch. 18 holes, par 72. Call 707-785-2468.

Sebastopol Golf Course, Sebastopol. Nine holes, par 66 for 18 holes. Call 707-823-9852.

Sonoma Mission Inn Golf Club. 18 holes, par 72. Call 707-996-0300.

Tayman Park Municipal Golf Course, Healdsburg. Nine holes, par 35. Call 707-433-4275.

Wikiup Golf Course, Santa Rosa. Nine holes, par 29. Call 707-546-8787.

Windsor Golf Club, Windsor. 18 holes, par 72. Call 707-838-7888.

## ICE SKATING

Redwood Empire Ice Arena (Snoopy's Home Ice). Call 707-546-7147.

## SPECTATOR SPORTS

Sonoma County Crushers' baseball season runs from May through September. At-home games at Rohnert Park Stadium. For schedule, tickets, or information call 707-588-8300.

## JUST LOOKING

## ART

Art Galleries and exhibitions are easy to find in Sonoma County. Every city has several galleries and many of the county's restaurants and wineries feature the works of local artists on a rotating basis. Each of the county's library branches hosts two art shows each year in their forum rooms. In addition, each city has regularly scheduled art walks and open studios. For information about what art is where during your stay, call the local Chambers of Commerce.

## MUSIC AND DRAMA

Santa Rosa Symphony, conductor Jeffrey Kahane, Luther Burbank Center, Santa Rosa. Call 707-546-7097.

Luther Burbank Center for the Arts, Santa Rosa. Popular venue for variety of music - classical to country. Call 707-546-3600.

Actors Theatre, Luther Burbank Center, Santa Rosa. Season runs October to August. Call 707-523-4185.

Charles M. Schultz Museum and Research Center, Santa Rosa. Call 707-579-4452

Cinnabar Theatre, Petaluma. Performs all year, special holiday programs and Summer Music Festival. Call 707-763-8920.

Santa Rosa Players, Santa Rosa. Season runs October through June. Call 707-544-7827.

## MUSEUMS

Healdsburg Museum, Healdsburg. Call 707-431-3325.

Jesse Peter Native American Art Museum, Santa Rosa. Call 707-527-4479.

Pacific Coast Air Museum, Charles M. Schultz Airport, Santa Rosa. Ongoing display of historic aircraft. Call 707-575-7900.

Petaluma Historical Library and Museum, Petaluma. Call 707-778-4398.

Sonoma County Museum, Santa Rosa. Permanent exhibit: Sonoma County: The Chosen Spot of All the Earth. Call 707-579-1500.

Sonoma Depot Museum, Sonoma. Permanent exhibit: replica of Bear Flag raising in Plaza, railway depot. Call 707-938-1762.

Sonoma Museum of Visual Art, Luther Burbank Center, Santa Rosa. Call 707-527-0297.

Sonoma Valley Museum of Art, Sonoma. Call 707-939-7862.

West County Museum, Sebastopol. Call 707-829-6711.

## BALLOONING

Vintage Aircraft Company, Sonoma. Scenic tours by vintage biplane. Call 707-938-2444.

Aeroventure Club, Petaluma. Lessons and scenic rides. Call 707-778-6767.

Aerostat Adventures Ballooning, Windsor. Call 707-433-3777.

Air Flambuoyant, Santa Rosa. Call 707-838-0333.

Hot Air and Co., Windsor/Healdsburg area. Call 707-823-6892.

## TOURING IN STYLE

Wine Country Carriages, Sebastopol. Backroads exploration and wine tasting in a 19th Century horse-drawn surrey. Call 707-823-7083.

California Wine Tours, Sonoma. Call 707-939-7225.

A Touch of Class Limousines, Santa Rosa. Call 707-539-0945.

## SPECIAL ATTRACTIONS

California Welcome Center, Rohnert Park. Interactive information kiosks, topographical maps, demonstration vineyard, wine-tasting, wine shop and gifts. Call 707-586-3795.

Fort Ross State Historic Park, Highway 1 at Fort Ross Road. Original settlement of Russian colonists in 1812. Restored structures, including chapel and stockade. Museum and gift shop. Call 707-847-3286.

Jack London State Historic Park, Glen Ellen. Hiking, nature trail, equestrian trail, self-guided history trail, author's grave, Wolf House ruins, museum. Open hours vary. Call 707-938-5216.

Luther Burbank Home and Gardens, National Historic Landmark, Santa Rosa. Home, gardens, greenhouse. Open hours vary. Call 707-524-5445.

Petaluma Adobe State Historic Park, Petaluma. Former headquarters of General Mariano Vallejo. Self-guided tour of dining area, workshop and living quarters, furnished and equipped with period furniture. Call 707-762-4871.

Sonoma State Historic Park, Sonoma. Historic structures include Mission San Francisco de Solano, army barracks once used to house General Vallejo's troops. West on Spain Street, General Vallejo's mansion and gardens, restored and furnished in the manner of the period. Call 707-938-9560.

Sonoma Train Town, Sonoma. 20-minute train trips on child-scale railroad, carousel, Ferris wheel, petting zoo. Call 707-996-2559.

Safari West, Santa Rosa. 400-acre wildlife preserve. On-site lodging available. Reservations required. Call 707-579-2552.

Santa Rosa Sailing Club. Events first Sunday of each month. Call 707-836-0717.

Paradise Ridge Sculpturegrove, Santa Rosa. A changing collection of large sculptures in a four-acre native oak environment. Call 707-528-9463.

Sonoma County Wine Library, Healdsburg. Counted among the finest wine libraries in the world. Collection of 5000 books, some dating back to 16th Century. For information or to join support group, Wine Library Associates of Sonoma County, call 707-433-3772.

Excellent sources for further exploration:

Russian River Wine Road map, available at all wineries, free, or call 800-723-6336.

Farm Trails map, available free at farm locations, or call 707-571-8288.

The
Wineries

## ADLER FELS

5325 Corrick Lane, Santa Rosa, CA 95409
Phone: 707-539-3123, Fax: 707-539-3128
E-mail: adlerfelswinery@yahoo.com
Website: www.adlerfels.com
Winery tours by appointment.
Tasting 11:00AM-4:00PM at The Wine Room,
9575 Sonoma Hwy., Kenwood, CA 95452. No fee.
Winemaker: David Coleman
Annual Case Production: 12,000

## ALDERBROOK VINEYARDS & WINERY

2306 Magnolia Drive, Healdsburg, CA 95448
Phone: 707-433-9154, 800-655-3838 Fax: 707-433-1862
Website: www.alderbrook.com
Tasting Room Hours: 10:00AM-5:00PM. No fee.
Picnic area, Gift Shop
Winemaker: T. J. Evans
Annual Case Production: 38,000

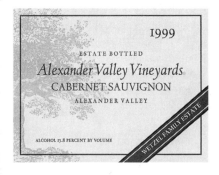

## ALEXANDER VALLEY VINEYARDS

8644 Highway 128, Healdsburg, CA 95448
Phone: 800-888-7209, Fax: 707-433-9408
E-mail: avv@avvwine.com
Website: www.avvwine.com
Tasting Room Hours: 10:00AM-5:00PM, daily.
Fee to taste Library Wines only. Refundable with
purchase. Picnic area. Tours of winery, caves,
historic sites, and gardens by appointment.
Winemaker: Kevin Hall
Annual Case Production: 100,000

## ANNAPOLIS WINERY
26055 Soda Springs Rd., Annapolis, CA 95412
Phone: 707-886-5460, Fax: 707-886-5460+5**
E-mail: barbarascalabrini@hotmail.com
Tasting Room Hours: 12:00 noon-5:00PM
No fee for tasting
Picnic area, gift shop, deli
Winemakers: Basil and Aron Scalabrini
Annual Case Production: 2,000

## ARMIDA WINERY
2201 Westside Rd., Healdsburg, CA 95448
Phone: 707-433-2222, Fax: 707-433-2202.
E-mail: wino@armida.com
Website: www.armida.com.
Tasting Room Hours: 11:00AM-5:00PM. No fee.
Picnic area, gift shop, gardens, bocce
Winemaker: Mike Loykasek
Annual Case Production: 10,000

## ARROWOOD VINEYARDS & WINERY
14347 Sonoma Hwy., Glen Ellen, CA 95442
Phone: 707-935-2600, Fax: 707-938-5947
Website: www.arrowoodvineyards.com.
Tasting Room Hours: 10:00AM-4:30PM.
Tasting Fee of $5.00 for Classics, $10.00
for Reserves. Gift Shop
Winemaker: Richard Arrowood, Wine Master
Annual Case Production: 30,000

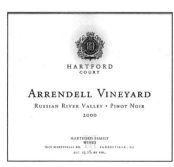

## ARTISAN CELLARS

337 Healdsburg Ave., Healdsburg, CA 95448
Phone: 707-433-7102
Tasting Room Hours: 10:00AM-5:00PM
$5.00 tasting fee refunded upon purchase.
Gift shop, and tasting of Villa Aceno,
Hartford Wines, Cambria, Verite and Archipel.

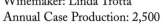

## BARTHOLOMEW PARK WINERY

1000 Vineyard Lane, Sonoma, CA 95476
Phone: 707-935-9511, Fax: 707-935-0549
E-mail: wines@bartholomewparkwinery.com
Website: www.bartholomewparkwinery.com
Tasting Room Hours: 11:00AM-4:30PM-$3.00 fee
Picnic area, gift shop, gardens, hiking trails, museum
Winemaker: Linda Trotta
Annual Case Production: 2,500

## BATTAGLINI ESTATE WINERY

2948 Piner Rd., Santa Rosa, CA 95401
Phone: 707-578-4091, Fax 650-588-4171
Tasting Room Hours: By Appointment. No fee.
Small picnic area
Winemaker: Joe Battaglini
Annual Case Production: 2,000

## BELVEDERE VINEYARDS & WINERY

4035 Westside Rd., Healdsburg, CA 95448
Phone: 800-433-8296, 707-431-4442, Fax: 707-431-0826
Website: www.belvederewinery.com
Tasting Room Hours: 11:00AM-5:00PM. No fee.
An acre Aroma Garden, wine by the glass. Jazz on the Deck,
Saturdays and Sundays, August-October. Picnic Terrace.
Winemaker: Bob Bertheau
Annual Case Production: 50,000

## BENZIGER FAMILY WINERY

1883 London Ranch Rd., Glen Ellen, CA 95442
Phone: 707-935-3000, 888-490-2739
Website: www.benziger.com
Tasting Room Hours: 10:00AM-5:00PM. No fee.
Gift shop, vineyard tram tour, self-guided tour,
Discovery Center, peacock aviary, picnic area.
Winemakers: Mike Benziger, Terry Nolan
Annual Case Production: 150,000

## BLACKSTONE WINERY SONOMA VALLEY

8450 Highway 12, Kenwood, CA 95452
Phone: 707-833-1999, 800-955-9585
Website: www.blackstonewinery.com
Tasting Room Hours: 10:00AM-4:30PM. No Fee.
Gift shop
Winemaker: Dennis Hill
Annual Case Production: 125,000

## BUENA VISTA HISTORIC WINERY and TASTING ROOM
18000 Old Winery Rd, P. O. Box 1842, Sonoma, CA 95476
Phone: 800-926-1266 Fax: 707-939-0916
E-mail: tastingroom@buenavistawinery.com
Tasting Room Hours: 10:00AM-5:00PM
No fee to taste current releases; $5.00 for older wines.
Historic rustic site with shade trees, creek, picnic area,
historic presentation.
Gift shop. Artist in residence.
Winemaker: Judy Matulich-Weitz
Annual Case Production: 450,000

## RAYMOND BURR VINEYARDS
8339 West Dry Creek Rd, Healdsburg, CA 95448
Phone: 707-433-4365, Fax: 707-431-1843
E-mail: Rbwyn@aol.com
Website: www.raymondburrvineyards.com
Tasting Room Hours: By appointment. No fee.
Picnic area on patio, wines and gifts for sale.
Winemaker: John Quinones
Annual Case Production: 3,000

## DAVIS BYNUM WINERY
8075 Westside Rd., Healdsburg, CA 95448
Phone: 707-433-2611, Fax: 707-433-4309
E-mail: info@davisbynum.com
Website: www.davisbynum.com
Tasting Room Hours: 10:00AM-5:00PM. No fee
Winemaker: David Georges
Annual Case Production: 13,000

CALE CELLARS
  16060 Sonoma Hwy., Sonoma, CA 95476
  Phone: 707-939-8363, Fax (same).
  E-mail: calewines@aol.com
  Tasting at The Wine Room, 9575 Sonoma Hwy., Kenwood
  11:00AM-5:00PM. No fee.
  Picnic area, gift shop
  Winemaker: Mike Cale
  Annual Case Production: 3,000

CAMELLIA CELLARS
  1048 Alexander Valley Rd., Healdsburg, CA 95448
  Phone: 888-404-9463, Fax: 707-433-1290
  Website: www.camelliacellars.com
  Tasting daily 11:00AM-6:00PM at Locals,
  21023 Geyserville Ave, Geyserville
  Winemaker: Bruce Snyder
  Annual Case Production: 2,000

CANYON ROAD WINERY
  19550 Geyserville Ave., Geyserville, CA 95441
  Phone: 800-793-9463, Fax: 707-857-9413.
  Website: www.canyonroadwinery.com
  Tasting Room Hours: 10:00AM-5:00PM. No fee.
  Picnic area, extensive gift shop, bocce court.
  Winemaker: Chris Munsell
  Annual Case Production: 290,000

## CHALK HILL ESTATE VINEYARDS & WINERY
10300 Chalk Hill Rd., Healdsburg, CA 95448
Phone: 707-838-4306, 800-838-4306, Fax 707-838-9687
Website: www.chalkhill.com
Tasting Room Hours: By appointment. Complimentary tours
and tasting at 10:00AM-4:00PM, Monday through Friday
Winemaker: Bill Knuttel
Assistant Winemaker: Lisa Bishop-Forbes
Annual Case Production: 75,000

## CHATEAU ST. JEAN WINERY
8555 Sonoma Hwy., P. O. Box 293, Kenwood, CA 95452
Phone: 707-833-4134, Fax: 707-833-5556
Website: www.chateaustjean.com
Tasting Room Hours: 10:00AM-6:00PM, May-October.
November-April, 10:00AM-5:00PM. $5.00 fee: $10.00
for three tastes of Reserve wines in Vineyard room.
Gardens, charcuterie, gift shop, picnic area, wine education;
Winemakers: Steve Reeder and Margo Van Staaveren.
Annual Case Production: 250,000 cases

## CHATEAU SOUVERAIN
400 Souverain Rd., P. O. Box 528, Geyserville, CA 95441
Phone: 888-809-4637 Fax: 707-857-4656
Website: www.chateausouverain.com
Tasting Room Hours: 10:00AM to 5:00PM.
$3.00 fee applies to purchase.
Gift shop, restaurant (see restaurant section)
Winemaker: Ed Killian
Annual Case Production: 150,000

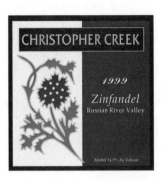

### CHRISTOPHER CREEK WINERY
641 Limerick Lane, Healdsburg, CA 95448
Phone: 707-433-2001. Fax: 707-431-0183
E-mail: chriscrk@ix.netcom.com
Website: www.christophercreek.com
Tasting Room Hours: 11:00AM-5:00PM,
Friday-Monday, or by Appointment. No fee.
Picnic area
Winemaker: Chris Russi
Annual Case Production: 4,000

### CLINE CELLARS
24737 Arnold Dr., Sonoma, CA 95476
Phone: 707-940-4000, Fax: 707-940-4033
Tasting Room Hours: 10:00AM-6:00PM. No fee.
Gift shop, picnic area, gardens, historical features.
Winemaker: Charles Tsegeletos
Annual Case Production: 180,000

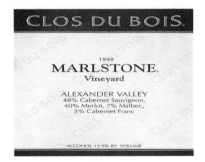

### CLOS DU BOIS WINES, INC.
19410 Geyserville Ave., Geyserville, CA 95441
Phone: 800-222-3189, 707-857-3100, Fax: 707-857-3229
Website: www.closdubois.com
Tasting Room Hours: 10:00AM-4:30PM. No fee.
Picnic area, cheese and deli meats, gift shop
Winemaker: Margaret Davenport
Annual Case Production: 1.4 million

## B. R. COHN WINERY

    15000 Sonoma Hwy., Glen Ellen, CA 95442
    Phone: 707-938-4064, Fax: 707-938-4585
    E-mail: linda@brcohn.com
    Website: www.b.r.cohn.com
    Tasting Room Hours: 10:00AM-5:00PM.
    Fee for tasting Reserve wines only.
    Picnic area, gift shop
    Winemaker: Mike Gulyash
    Annual Case Production: 18,000

## DEERFIELD RANCH WINERY

    1310 Warm Springs Rd, Glen Ellen, CA 95442
    Phone: 707-833-5215, Fax: 707-833-1312.
    E-mail: winery@deerfieldranch.com
    Website: www.deerfield.com
    Tasting Room Hours: 11:00AM-6:00PM
    at Family Wineries Tasting Room. No fee.
    9200 Sonoma Hwy., Kenwood, CA 95452
    Winemakers: Robert Rex, Michael Browne, assistant.
    Annual Case Production: 7,500

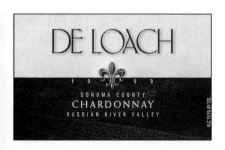

## DE LOACH VINEYARDS

    1791 Olivet Rd., Santa Rosa, CA 95401
    Phone: 707-526-9111, Fax: 707-526-4151
    Website: www.deloachvineyards.com
    Tasting Room Hours: 10:00AM-4:30PM. No fee.
    Gift shop, art by local artists, picnic area.
    Winemaker: Dan Cederquist
    Annual Case Production: 250,000

## DeLORIMIER WINERY

2001 Hwy 128, Geyserville, CA 95441
Phone: 800-546-7718, Fax: 707-857-3262
E-mail: discover@delorimierwinery.com
Website: www.delorimierwinery.com
Tasting Room Hours: 10:00AM-4:30PM. No fee
Picnic area, Russian River access.
Winemaker: Don Frazer
Annual Case Production: 12,000

## DRY CREEK VINEYARD

3770 Lambert Bridge Rd., Healdsburg, CA 95448
Phone: 707-433-1000, 800-864-9463, Fax 707-433-5329
E-mail: dcv@drycreekvineyard.com
Website: www.drycreekvineyard.com
Tasting Room Hours: 10:30AM-4:30PM.
Picnic area, gift shop, gardens. Four tastes free.
Winemaker: Jeff McBride
Annual Case Production: 130,000

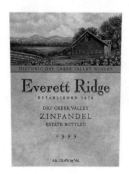

## EVERETT RIDGE VINEYARDS & WINERY, LLC

435 West Dry Creek Rd., Healdsburg, CA 95448
Phone: 707-433-1637, Fax 707-433-7024
E-mail: info@everettridge.com
Website: www.everettridge.com
Tasting Room Hours: 11:00AM to 4:00PM. No fee.
Picnic tables with spectacular view, gift shop
Winemaker: John Allen Burtner
Annual Case Production: 7,000

## FERRARI-CARANO VINEYARDS AND WINERY
8761 Dry Creek Rd., Healdsburg, CA 95448
Phone: 707-433-6700, Fax: 707-431-1742
Website: www.ferrari-carano.com
Tasting Room Hours: 10:00AM-5:00PM. $3.00 fee,
refundable with wine purchase.
Magnificent gardens, views, underground cellar, gift shop.
Winemaker: George Bursick
Annual Case Production: 150,000

## FIELD STONE WINERY & VINEYARD
10075 Hwy 128, Healdsburg, CA 95448
Phone: 707-433-7266, Fax 707-433-2231
Website: www.fieldstone.com
Tasting Room Hours: 10:00AM-5:00PM. No fee.
Wines available by the glass.
Two picnic areas, cheese, sausage and crackers.
Winemaker: Tom Milligan
Annual Case Production: 10,000 cases

## FOPPIANO VINEYARDS
12707 Old Redwood Hwy., Healdsburg, CA 95448
Phone: 707-433-7272, Fax: 707-433-0565
E-mail: lfoppiano@aol.com
Website: www.foppiano.com
Tasting Room Hours: 10:00AM-4:30PM. No fee.
Picnic area, gift shop, self-guided vineyard tour.
Winemaker: Bill Regan
Annual Case Production: 85,000

## FORCHINI VINEYARDS & WINERY

5141 Dry Creek Rd., Healdsburg, CA 95448
Phone: 707-431-8886, Fax: 707-431-8881
E-mail: wine@forchini.com
Website: www.forchini.com
Tasting Room Hours: By appointment.
Winemaker: Jim Forchini
Annual Case Production: 3,000

## FRICK

23072 Walling Rd., Geyserville, CA 95441
Phone: 707-857-3205, Fax: 707-857-3205
E-mail: frick@frickwinery.com
Website: www.frickwinery.com
Tasting Room Hours: Saturday and Sunday,
12:00PM-4:30PM
No Fee. Lounging porch, gift shop, art.
Winemaker: Bill Frick
Annual Case Production: 2,500

## GEYSER PEAK WINERY

22281 Chianti Rd., Geyserville CA 95441
Phone: 800-255-9463, Fax: 707-857-9402
Website: www.geyserpeakwinery.com
Tasting Room Hours: 10:00AM-5:00PM.
Fee for tasting reserve wines.
Picnic area, gift shop
Winemakers: Daryl Groom, Mick Schroeter,
Chris Munsell, Ondine Chattan
Annual Case Production: 280,000

## GLORIA FERRER CHAMPAGNE CAVES

23555 Hwy 121, P. O. Box 1427, Sonoma, CA 95476
Phone: 707-996-7256, Fax: 707-996-7256
E-mail: tom@gloriaferrer.com
Website: www.gloriaferrer.com
Tasting Room Hours: 10:30AM-5:30PM.
Tasting fee $3.50 to $6.50 per glass.
Terrace seating. Small gift shop
Winemaker: Robert Iantosca
Annual Case Production: 115,000

## GUNDLACH-BUNDSCHU WINERY

2000 Denmark St., Sonoma, CA 95476.
Phone: 707-938-5277, Fax: 707-938-9460.
E-mail: info@gunbun.com.
Website: www.gunbun.com
Tasting Room Hours: 11:00AM-4:30PM. No fee.
Picnic area, summer Shakespeare Festival
Winemaker: Linda Trotta
Annual Case Production: 50,000

## HANNA WINERY, INC.

9280 Hwy 128, Healdsburg, CA 95448
Phone: 707-431-4310, Fax: 707-431-4314
5353 Occidental Rd., Santa Rosa, CA 95401
Website: www.hannawinery.com
Tasting Room Hours: 10:00AM-4:30PM, daily.
Both sites: Picnic area, gifts, local art
Winemaker: Jefferson Hinchliffe
Annual Case Production: 35,000

**HARTFORD FAMILY WINERY**
8075 Martinelli Rd., Forestville, CA 95436
Phone: 707-887-1756, Fax: 707-887-7158
Website: www.hartfordwines.com
Tasting Room Hours: 10:00AM-4:30PM.
Tasting fee, $5.00
Gardens, picnic tables
Winemaker: Mike Sullivan
Annual Case Production: 15,000

**HAWLEY WINES**
6387 West Dry Creek Rd., Healdsburg, CA 95448
Phone: 707-431-2705, Fax: 707-431-2705
E-mail: jhwines@aol.com
Website: www.hawleywine.com
Tasting daily 11:00AM-6:00PM at Locals,
21023 Geyserville Ave, Geyserville. Wine sales
direct by mail or phone. No credit cards accepted.
Winemaker: John Hawley
Annual Case Production: 3,000

**HOP KILN WINERY at GRIFFIN VINEYARD**
6050 Westside Rd., Healdsburg, CA 95448
Phone: 707-433-6491, Fax: 707-433-8162
E-mail: info@hopkilnwinery.com
Website: www.hopkilnwinery.com
Tasting Room Hours: 10:00AM-5:00PM.
No fee for current vintages; $2.00 fee for tasting reserve wines.
Picnic area by wildlife pond, gift shop, art gallery
Winemaker: Steve Strobl
Annual Case Production: 10,000

## IMAGERY ESTATE WINERY

14335 Sonoma Hwy., Glen Ellen, CA 95442
Phone: 707-935-4515, 877-550-4278
Website: www.imagerywinery.com
Tasting Room Hours: 10:00AM-4:30PM. No fee.
Gift Shop, art gallery, picnic area, gardens,
bocce court.
Winemaker: Joe Benziger
Annual Case Production: 7,000

## IRON HORSE VINEYARDS

9786 Ross Station Rd., Sebastopol, CA 95472
Phone: 707-887-1507, Fax: 707-887-1337
Website: www.ironhorsevineyards.com
Tasting Room Hours: By appointment, 10:00-3:30PM
Winemakers: Forrest Tancer and David Munksgard
Annual Case Production: 40,000

## J WINE COMPANY

11447 Old Redwood Hwy., Healdsburg, CA 95448
Phone: 707-431-3646, Fax: 707-431-5410
E-mail: winefolk@wine.com
Tasting Room Hours: 11:00AM-5:00PM.
Tastings served with food pairings: $3.00-$5.00
for a single wine tasting, and $8.00-$10.00 for a flight.
Gardens, gift shop
Winemaker: Oded Shakked
Annual Case Production: 45,000

## JOHNSON'S ALEXANDER VALLEY WINES

8333 Highway 128, Healdsburg, CA 95448
Phone: 707-433-2319, Fax: 707-433-5302
Website: www.johnsonwines.com
Tasting Room Hours: 10:00AM-5:00PM. No fee.
Picnic grounds, private parties, 1924 Robert Morton
Theatre Pipe Organ in tasting room.
Winemaker: Ellen Johnson
Annual Case Production: 2,000

## JORDAN VINEYARD & WINERY

1474 Alexander Valley Rd., Healdsburg, CA 95448
Phone: 707-431-5250, Fax: 707-431-5259
E-mail: publicrelations@jordancos.com
Retail sales only, 8:00AM-5:00PM, Monday-Friday;
9:00AM-4:00PM Saturday. Tours, with tasting,
by appointment.
Winemaker: Rob Davis
Annual Case Production: 85,000

## KENDALL-JACKSON WINE ESTATES

5007 Fulton Rd., Fulton, CA 95439
Phone: 707-571-8100, Fax: 707-546-9221
Website: www.kj.com
Tasting Room Hours: 10:00AM-5:00PM. $2.00 fee.
Picnic area, gift shop, tours of organic gardens.
Winemaker: Randy Ullom

## KENWOOD VINEYARDS

9592 Sonoma Hwy., P. O. Box 447, Kenwood, CA 95452
Phone: 707-833-5891, Fax: 707-833-6572
E-mail: info@kenwoodvineyards.com
Website: www.kenwoodvineyards.com
Tasting Room Hours: 10:00AM -4:30PM. No fee.
Gift Shop, food and wine tastings monthly.
 Winemaker: Michael Lee
Annual Case Production: 550,000

## KORBEL CHAMPAGNE CELLARS

13250 River Rd., Guerneville, CA 95446
Phone: 707-824-7000, Fax: 707-869-2506
E-mail: info@korbel.com
Website: www.korbel.com
Tasting Room Hours: 9:00AM-5:00PM, May through
September; 9:00AM-4:30PM, October-April. No fee.
Winery tours start 10:00AM. Garden tours, 11:00, 1:00,
and 3:00 April 15-October 15. Delicatessen open daily.
Winemaker: Paul Ahvenainen
Annual Case Production: 1.6 million

## KUNDE ESTATE WINERY & VINEYARDS

10155 Sonoma Hwy, P. O. Box 639, Kenwood, CA 95452
Phone: 707-833-5501, Fax: 707-833-2204
E-mail: wineinfo@kunde.com
Website: www.kunde.com
Tasting Room Hours: 10:30AM-4:30PM. No Fee.
Shaded picnic grounds, gift shop
Winemaker: David Noyes
Annual Case Production: 130,000

## LAKE SONOMA WINERY

9990 Dry Creek Rd., Geyserville, CA 95441
Phone: 707-473-2999, Fax: 707-431-8356
E-mail : info@lswinery.com
Website: www.lakesonomawinery.net
Tasting Room Hours: 10:00AM-5:00PM. No fee.
Picnic area on veranda overlooking the entire
Dry Creek Valley. Gift shop.
Winemaker: Chris Wills
Annual Case Production: 16,000

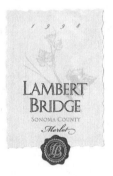

## LAMBERT BRIDGE WINERY

4085 W. Dry Creek Rd., Healdsburg, CA 95448
Phone: 800-975-0555, Fax: 707-433-3215.
E-mail: wines@lambertbridge.com
Website: www.lambertbridge.com
Tasting Room Hours: 10:30AM-4:30PM. No fee.
Picnic garden, gift shop.
Winemaker: Julia Iantosca
Annual Case Production: 20,000

## LANDMARK VINEYARDS

101 Adobe Canyon Rd., P. O. Box 340, Kenwood, CA 95452
Phone: 800-452-6365, Fax: 707-833-0053
E-mail: overlook@landmarkwine.com
Website: www.landmarkwine.com
Tasting Room Hours: 10:00AM-4:30PM. No fee,
except for tasting Reserve wines.
Wine Club: 800-452-6365, Ext. 226.
Picnic area, gift shop, gardens, bocce court
Winemaker: Eric Stern
Annual Case Production: 20,000

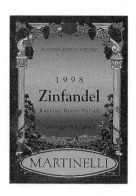

MARTINELLI WINERY
3360 River Rd., Windsor, CA 95492
Phone:707-525-0570, Fax: 707-525-9463
Tasting Room Hours: 10:00AM-5:00PM. No fee.
Gift shop, apples and pumpkins in season.
Picnic area
Winemakers: Helen Turley, Bryan Kvamme, assistant
Annual Case Production: 12,000

MARTINI & PRATI WINERY
2191 Laguna Rd., Santa Rosa, CA 95401
Phone: 707-823-2404, Fax: 707-829-6151
Tasting Room Hours: 11:00AM-5:00PM. No Fee.
Picnic area, Italian Groceria, tours of historic winery
Winemaker: Terri Strain
Annual Case Production: 6,000

MATANZAS CREEK WINERY
6097 Bennett Valley Rd., Santa Rosa, CA 95404
Phone: 800-590-6464, Fax: 707-571-0156
E-mail: info@matanzascreek.com
Website: www.matanzascreek.com
Tasting Room Hours: 10:00AM-4:30PM.
Fee for tasting, $5.00 a flight, refunded with wine purchase.
Picnic area, sculptures, lavender fields, gardens.
Annual Case Production: 40,000

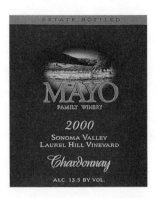

**MAYO FAMILY WINERY**
No visitors permitted at winery.
Wines may be tasted 11:00AM-6:00PM at
Family Wineries of Sonoma, 9200 Sonoma Hwy.,
Kenwood, CA 95452 and The Cellar Door,
1395 Broadway, Sonoma, CA 95476. No fee.
Phone: 707-833-5504, Fax: 707-833-6550.
Winemaker: Chris Stanton
Annual Case Production: 3,500

**MAZZOCCO VINEYARDS**
1400 Lytton Springs Rd., Healdsburg, CA 95448
Phone: 707-433-9035, 707-431-8159. Fax 707-431-2369
E-mail: vino@mazzocco.com
Website: www.mazzocco.com
Tasting Room Hours: 10:00AM-4:30PM. No fee.
Small picnic area, large gift shop, bocce court
Winemaker: Phyllis Zouzounis
Annual Case Production: 17,000

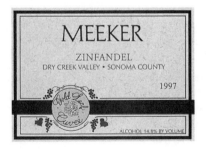

**THE MEEKER VINEYARD**
21035 Geyserville Ave., P. O. Box 215, Geyserville, CA 95441
Phone: 707-431-2148, Fax: 707-431-2549
E-mail: cmmeek@aol.com
Tasting Room Hours: 10:30AM-5:00PM. No fee.
Winemakers: Matt Blankenheim
Annual Case Production: 6,000

## MICHEL-SCHLUMBERGER WINE ESTATE

4155 Wine Creek Rd., Healdsburg, CA 95448.
Phone: 800-447-3060, 707-433-7427. Fax: 707-433-0444
E-mail: wine@michelschlumberger.com
Website: www.michelschlumberger.com
Tours by appointment daily. No charge for tours.
Custom tours also available.
Winemaker: Fred Payne
Annual Case Production: 25,000.

## MILL CREEK VINEYARDS & WINERY

1401 Westside Rd., P. O. Box 758, Healdsburg, CA 95448
Phone: 707-431-2121, Fax: 707-431-1714
E-mail: tr@mcvonline.com
Website: www.mcvonlline.com
Tasting Room Hours: 10:00AM-5:00PM. No fee.
Two picnic areas: one overlooking Dry Creek Valley; one
by the water wheel pond. Self-guided native plant walk.
Winemaker: Hank Skewis
Annual Case Production: 15,000

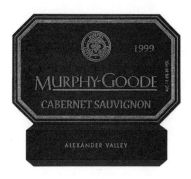

## MURPHY-GOODE ESTATE WINERY

4001 Hwy. 128, P. O. Box 158, Geyserville, CA 95441
Phone: 707-431-7644, Fax: 707-431-8640
E-mail: general@murphygoodewinery.com
Website: www.murphygoodewinery.com
Tasting Room Hours: 10:30AM-4:30PM. No fee.
Gift Shop
Winemaker: David Ready Jr.
Annual Case Production: 150,000

## NALLE WINERY

2383 Dry Creek Rd., P. O. Box 454, Healdsburg, CA 95448
Phone: 707-433-1040, Fax: 707-433-6062
E-mail: dbnalle@sonic.net
Website: www.nallewinery.com
Tours by appointment.
Winemaker: Doug Nalle
Annual Case Production: 2,000

## NELSON ESTATE

Office Address: P. O. Box 66067, Seattle, WA 98166
Phone: 206-241-9463
Website: www.nelsonestate.com
No fee tasting, 11:00AM-6:00PM at Family Wineries
9200 Sonoma Hwy., Kenwood, CA 95452,
Phone: 707-833-5504
Winemaker: Alison Green Doran
Annual Case Production: 3,000

## PARADISE RIDGE WINERY

4545 Thomas Lake Harris Dr., Santa Rosa, CA 95403
Phone: 707-528-9463, Fax: 707-528-9481
E-mail: info@prwinery.com
Website: www.paradiseridgewinery.com
Tasting Room Hours: 11:00AM-5:30PM. No fee.
Sculpture grove, art displays, gifts.
Kanaye Nagasawa historical exhibit.
Winemaker: Dan Barwick
Annual Case Production: 5,000

**PASTORI WINERY**
  23189 Geyserville Ave., Cloverdale, CA 95425
  Phone: 707-857-3418
  Tasting Room Hours: 9:00AM-5:00PM. No fee.
  Winemaker: Frank Pastori
  Annual Case Production: 1,000

**PEDRONCELLI WINERY**
  1220 Canyon Rd., Geyserville, CA 95441
  Phone: 707-857-3531, 800-836-3894, Fax: 707-857-3812
  E-mail: service@pedroncelli.com
  Website: www.pedroncelli.com
  Tasting Room Hours: 10:00AM-4:30PM. No fee.
  Picnic area, small gift shop, art exhibits, bocce court.
  Winemaker: John Pedroncelli
  Annual Case Production: 80,000

**PEZZI KING VINEYARDS & GARDENS**
  3805 Lambert Bridge Rd., Healdsburg, CA 95448
  Phone: 800-411-4758, Fax: 707-431-9389.
  Website: www.pezziking.com
  Tasting Room Hours: 10:00AM-4:30PM. No fee.
  Beautiful picnic pavilions in garden setting. Gift shop.
  Winemaker: Tim Crowe
  Annual Case Production: 18,000

## PORTER CREEK VINEYARDS
8735 Westside Rd., Healdsburg, CA 95448
Phone: 707-433-6321, Fax: 707-433-4245
E-mail: dijon1@sonic.net
Tasting Room Hours: Summer: 10:30AM-4:30PM daily.
Winter, same hours, Wednesday-Monday. No fee.
Winemaker: Alex Davis
Annual Case Production: 3,500

## PRESTON OF DRY CREEK (PRESTON VINEYARDS)
9282 West Dry Creek Rd., Healdsburg, CA 95448
Phone: 707-433-3372, Fax: 707-433-5307
E-mail: mail@prestonvineyards.com
Website: www.prestonvineyards.com
Tasting Room Hours: 11:00AM-4:30PM. No fee.
No groups of more than eight, please.
Picnic area, gardens.
Winemaker: Lou Preston
Annual Case Production: 8,000

## QUIVIRA ESTATE VINEYARDS AND WINERY
4900 West Dry Creek Rd., Healdsburg, CA 95448
Phone: 707-431-8333, Fax: 707-431-1664.
E-mail: quivira@quivirawine.com
Website: www.quivirawine.com
Tasting Room Hours: 11:00AM-5:00PM. No fee.
Picnic area.
Winemaker: Grady Wann
Annual Case Production: 20,000

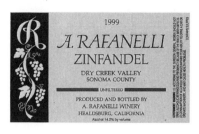

**A. RAFANELLI WINERY & VINEYARD**
4685 West Dry Creek Rd., Healdsburg, CA 95448
Phone: 707-433-1385
Tasting and sales by appointment. No fee.
No credit cards accepted.
Two picnic tables.
Winemaker: Rashell Rafanelli-Fehlman
Annual Case Production: 10,000

**RAVENSWOOD WINERY**
18701 Gehricke Rd., Sonoma, CA 95476
Phone: 707-933-2332, Fax 707-938-9459.
E-mail: rwwine@ravenswood-wine.com
Website: www.ravenswood-wine.com
Tasting Room Hours: 10:00AM-4:30PM. $4.00 tasting fee.
Gift shop. Tours by prior reservation at 10:30AM.
Winemaker: Joel Peterson
Annual Case Production: 500,000

**ROCHE CARNEROS ESTATE WINERY**
28700 Arnold Dr., Sonoma, CA 95476.
Phone: 707-935-7115, Fax: 707-935-7846.
E-mail: info@rochewinery.com
Website: www.rochewinery.com
Tasting Room Hours: 10:00AM-6:00PM.
No fee to taste current releases. $3.00 for Reserves.
Gift shop, small picnic area with great view.
Winemaker: Michael Carr
Annual Case Production: 8,000

## ROCHIOLI VINEYARD & WINERY
6192 Westside Rd., Healdsburg, CA 95448
Phone:707-433-2305, Fax: 707-433-2358
Tasting Room Hours: 11:00AM-4:00PM. No fee.
Small gift shop, picnic area overlooking vineyard.
Winemaker: Tom Rochioli
Annual Case Production: 10,000

## RUSSIAN HILL ESTATE WINERY
4525 Slusser Rd., Windsor, CA 95492
Phone: 707-575-9428, Fax: 707-575-9453
E-mail: russianhillestate@att.net
Website: www.russianhillwinery.com
Tasting room scheduled to open January 2003
Winemaker: Patrick Melley
Annual Case Production: 5,000

## SABLE RIDGE VINEYARDS
6320 Jamison Rd., Santa Rosa, CA 95404
Phone: 707-542-3138, Fax: 707-542-8668
E-mail: sableridge@aol.com
Website: www.sableridge.com
Tours and tasting at winery by appointment. Tasting at
Family Tasting Room, 9200 Sonoma Hwy., Kenwood,
11:00AM-6:00PM. No fee. Phone: 707-833-5504.
Winemaker: Kevin Hamel
Annual Case Production: 4,000.

**SAINT FRANCIS WINERY & VINEYARDS**
100 Pythian Rd., Santa Rosa, CA 95409
Phone: 800-543-7713, Fax: 707-833-6146
Website: www.stfranciswine.com
Tasting Room Hours: 10:00AM-5:00PM.
Fee for tasting, $5.00. Mission style tasting
center, two tasting rooms, gift shop.
Winemaker: Tom Mackey
Annual Case Production: 200,000

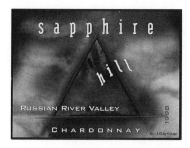

**SAPPHIRE HILL VINEYARDS**
40 Mill St., Healdsburg, CA 95448
Phone and Fax: 707-838-3245
Website: www.sapphirehill.com
Tasting by appointment, and during
major local wine events.
Winemaker: Greg LaFollette
Annual Case Production: 4,000

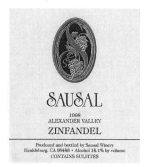

**SAUSAL WINERY**
7370 Hwy. 128, Healdsburg, CA 95448
Phone: 707-433-2285, Fax: 707-433-5136
E-mail: zinfanz@sonic.net
Website: www.sausalwinery.com
Tasting Room Hours: 10:00AM-4:00PM. No fee.
Picnic area
Winemaker: Dave Demostene
Annual Case Production: 10,000

## SCHUG CARNEROS ESTATE WINERY
602 Bonneau Rd., Sonoma, CA 95476.
Phone: 800-966-9365, Fax: 707-939-9364.
E-mail: schug@schugwinery.com
Website: www.schugwinery.com
Tasting Room Hours: 10:00AM-5:00PM. No fee to
taste current releases, $5.00 for Heritage Reserve wines.
Cave tours by appointment, picnic tables, petanque court
Winemakers: Walter Schug, winemaster,
Michael Cox, winemaker.
Annual Case Production: 20,000

## SEBASTIANI VINEYARDS & WINERY
389 Fourth St. East, P. O. Box AA, Sonoma, CA 95476
Phone: 707-933-3200. Fax: 707-933-3370
Tasting Room Hours: 10:00AM-5:00PM.
$6.00 tasting fee includes logo glass. Private
tastings by appointment. Wine and food events.
Picnic areas, tours, gift shop, gardens, trolley.
Winemaker: Mark Lyon
Annual Case Production: 150,000

## SEBASTIANI ON THE SQUARE
40 West Spain St., Sonoma, CA 95476
Phone: 707-933-3290, Fax: 707-935-4484
Tasting Room Hours: 11:00AM-8:00PM Sunday-Wednesday:
11:00AM-9:00PM Thursday - Saturday.
Tasting fee with logo glass.
Extensive gift shop featuring wine country theme.

## SEBASTOPOL VINEYARDS
8757 Green Valley Rd., Sebastopol, CA 95472
Phone: 707-829-9463, Fax: 707-829-5368
E-mail: info@sebastopolvineyards.com
Website: www.sebastopolvineyards.com
Tasting Room Hours: Thursday through Monday,
11:00AM to 4:00PM. No fee.
Picnic area, gift shop
Winemaker: Merry Edwards
Annual Case Production: 5,000

## SEGHESIO FAMILY VINEYARDS
14730 Grove St., Healdsburg, CA 95448
Phone: 707-433-7764, Fax: 707-433-8495
E-mail: amy@seghesio.com
Website: www.seghesio.com
Tasting Room Hours: 10:00AM-4:30PM. No fee.
Picnic area, gift shop.
Winemaker: Ted Seghesio
Annual Case Production: 60,000

## SELBY WINERY
215 Center St., Healdsburg, CA 95448
Phone: 707-431-1703, Fax: 707-431-0439.
E-mail: selby@selbywinery.com
Tasting Room Hours: 11:00AM-5:00PM,
Friday - Monday, or by appointment. No fee.
Winemaker: Susie Selby
Annual Case Production: 7,500

## SILVER OAK CELLARS, ALEXANDER VALLEY
24625 Chianti Rd., Geyserville, CA 95441.
Phone: 800-273-8809, Fax: 707-944-2817.
Website: www.silveroak.com
Tasting Hours: 9:00AM-4:00PM, Monday-Saturday.
Tours by appointment only. $10.00 tasting fee;
Taster keeps special Silver Oak Glass.
Gift Shop, courtyard with fountain.
Winemaker: Daniel H. Baron
Annual Case Production (at this facility) 50,000

## SIMI WINERY
16275 Healdsburg Ave., Healdsburg, CA 95448
Phone: 707-433-6981, Fax: 707-433-6253
Website: www.simiwinery.com
Tasting Room Hours: 10:00AM-5:00PM. $5.00 fee
to taste four classics, $7.00 for three Reserves. Refunded with
purchase. Complimentary tours, March -November, 11:00AM,
1:00 and 3:00PM; 11:00AM, 2:00PM, December-February.
Winemakers: Nick Goldschmidt, David Ostheimer,
Susan Lueker
Annual Case Production: 200,000

## SMOTHERS WINERY/REMICK RIDGE VINEYARDS
No visitors permitted at winery.
Phone: 707-833-1010
Wines may be tasted 11:00AM-5:00PM, for no fee,
At The Wine Room, 9575 Sonoma Hwy.,
Kenwood, CA 95452.
Phone: 707-833-6131.
Winemaker: Richard Arrowood
Annual Case Production: 10,000

**SONOMA-CUTRER VINEYARDS**
    4401 Slusser Rd., Windsor, CA 95492
    Phone: 707-528-1181
    E-mail: info@sonomacutrer.com
    Website: www.sonomacutrer.com
    Tasting Room Hours: By Appointment. No fee.
    Open for sales 9:00AM-5:00PM
    Picnics allowed.
    Winemaker: Terry Adams
    Annual Case Production: 100,000

**STONE CREEK WINES**
    9380 Sonoma Hwy., Kenwood, CA 95452
    Phone: 707-833-4455, Fax: 707-833-1355
    Website: www.stonecreekwines.com
    Tasting Room Hours: 10:30AM-5:00PM. No fee.
    Gift shop, picnic area and garden
    Winemaker: Erin Green
    Annual Case Production: 130,000

**RODNEY STRONG VINEYARDS**
    11455 Old Redwood Hwy, Healdsburg, CA 95448.
    Phone: 707-431-1533, Fax: 707-433-0921
    Tasting Room Hours: 10:00AM-5:00PM. No fee.
    Tours: 11:00AM and 3:00PM, Picnic area, gift shop,
    Summer Concert Series.
    Winemaker: Rick Sayre
    Annual Case Production: 450,000

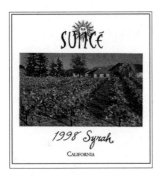

**SUNCÉ WINERY**
    1839 Olivet Rd., Santa Rosa, CA 95401
    Phone: 707-526-9463, Fax: 707-823-9106
    Tasting Room Hours: 11:00AM-5:00PM. No fee.
    Winemaker: Frane Franicevic
    Annual Case Production: 2,000

**JOSEPH SWAN VINEYARDS**
    2916 Laguna Rd., Forestville, CA 95436
    Phone: 707-573-3747, Fax: 707-575-1605
    E-mail: rod@swanwinery.com
    Tasting Room Hours: Saturday and Sunday,
    11:00AM-4:30PM. No fee.
    Winemaker: Rod Berglund
    Annual Case Production: 4,500

**TAFT STREET WINERY**
    2030 Barlow Ln., Sebastopol, CA 95472.
    Phone: 800-334-8238, Fax: 707-823-8622.
    E-mail: taftst@sonic.net
    Tasting Room Hours: 11:00AM-4:00PM, Monday
    through Friday, 11:00AM-4:30PM, weekends. No fee.
    Winemaker: John Tierney
    Annual Case Production: 60,000

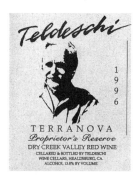

F. TELDESCHI WINERY
> 3555 Dry Creek Rd., Healdsburg, CA 95448
> Phone: 707-433-6626, Fax: 707-433-3077
> Tasting Room Hours: 11:30AM-5:30PM, daily,
> May-November. December-April, weekdays,
> 1:00-5:00PM. Noon to 5:00PM,
> weekends and holidays. Logo gift items.
> Winemaker: Dan Teldeschi
> Annual Case Production: 2,000

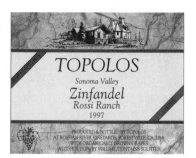

TOPOLOS AT RUSSIAN RIVER VINEYARDS
> 5700 Gravenstein Hwy. No., Forestville, CA 95436
> Phone: 707-887-1139, 800-867-6567
> E-mail: topolos@topolos.com
> Website: www.topolos.com
> Tasting Room Hours; 11:00AM-5:30PM. No fee.
> Gift shop, restaurant, aviaries.
> Winemaker: Jac Jacobs
> Annual Case Production: 18,000

MARIMAR TORRES
> 11400 Graton Rd, Sebastopol, CA 95472
> Phone: 707-823-4365, Fax: 707-823-4496.
> E-mail: marimar@marimarstate.com
> Website: www.marimarestate.com
> Tours and Tasting by appointment only.
> Marimar Torres, winegrower; Bill Dyer, Technical Director.
> Annual Case Production: 15,000

## TRENTADUE WINERY
19170 Geyserville Ave., Geyserville, CA 95441
Phone: 707-433-3104, Fax: 707-433-5825
Website: www.trentadue.com
Tasting Room Hours: 10:00AM-5:00PM. No fee.
$5.00 for Reserve tasting.
Winery has picnic areas, gardens, gift shop, special
events center. Plaza tasting room has gift shop.
Winemaker: Miro Tcholakov
Annual Case Production: 20,000

## VALLEY OF THE MOON WINERY
777 Madrone Rd., P. O. Box 1951, Glen Ellen, CA 95442
Phone: 707-996-6941, Fax: 707-996-7943
E-mail: luna@vomwinery.com
Website: www.valleyofthemoonwinery.com
Tasting Room Hours: 10:00AM-4:30PM. No fee.
Gift shop with unique items.
Winemaker: Pat Henderson
Annual Case Production: 35,000

## VIANSA WINERY & ITALIAN MARKETPLACE
25200 Arnold Dr., Sonoma, CA 95476
Phone: 707-935-4700, Fax: 707-996-4632
E-mail: tuscan@viansa.com
Website: www.viansa.com
Tasting Room Hours: 10:00AM-5:00PM.
Public Tours 11:00AM-1:00PM daily.
Four complimentary tastes, self-guided tours, picnic area,
Italian marketplace, BBQ (summer), Deli, wetlands.
Winemaker: Sam Sebastiani
Annual Case Production: N/A

## WELLINGTON VINEYARDS
11600 Dunbar Rd., Glen Ellen, CA 95442
Phone: 707-939-0780, 800-816-9463, Fax: 707-939-0378
E-mail: peter@wellingtonvineyards.com
Tasting Room Hours: 11:00AM-5:00PM. No fee.
Picnic area, gift shop
Winemaker: Peter Wellington
Annual Case Production: 7,000

## WHITE OAK VINEYARDS & WINERY
7505 Hwy.128, Healdsburg, CA 95448
Phone: 707-433-8429, Fax: 707-433-8446
Website: www.whiteoakwines.com
Tasting Room Hours: 10:00AM-5:00PM.
No fee to taste current releases.
Picnic grounds, tours by appointment, gifts.
Facility rental for groups.
Winemaker: Steve Ryan
Annual Case Production: 15,000

## WILD HOG VINEYARD
P. O. Box 189, Cazadero, CA 95421
Phone: 707-847-3687
No tasting room. Wines may be ordered by phone.
No credit cards accepted.
Winemaker: Daniel Schoenfeld
Annual Case Production: 3,000

WILSON WINERY

1960 Dry Creek Road, Healdsburg, CA 95448
Phone: 707-433-4355, fax 707-433-4353
E-mail: info@wilsonwinery.com
Website: www.wilsonwinery.com
Tasting Room Hours: Friday, Saturday,
Sunday 11:00 am - 5:00 pm. No fee.
Charming picnic area overlooking the vineyards
Name of winemakers: Ken and Diane Wilson
Annual case production: 7,000

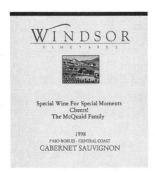

WINDSOR VINEYARDS

P. O. Box 368, Windsor, CA 95492
Phone: 707-836-5000. Wine orders 800-333-9987.
Fax: 707-836-5900
Website: www.windsorvineyards.com
Tasting Room: 308B Center St., Healdsburg, CA 95448
Monday-Friday, 10:00AM-5:00PM, Saturday and
Sunday, 10:00AM-6:00PM. No fee.
Tasting room phone: 707-433-2822. Wines, gifts.
Winemaker: Toni Stockhausen
Annual Case Production: 200,000

YOAKIM BRIDGE VINEYARDS & WINERY

7209 Dry Creek Rd., Healdsburg, CA 95448.
Phone: 707-433-8511, Fax: 707-431-9270
E-mail: virginia@yoakimbridge.com
Website: www.yoakimbridge.com
Tasting Room Hours: Weekends, 11:00AM-4:00PM.
Weekdays by appointment only. No fee.
Winemaker: David Cooper
Annual Case Production: 2,500

# Tasting Notes

# Tasting Notes

_____

_____

_____

_____

_____

_____

_____

_____

_____

_____

_____

_____

_____

_____

_____

# Tasting Notes

# Tasting Notes

# Tasting Notes

---
---
---
---
---
---
---
---
---
---
---
---
---
---
---
---
---

# Tasting Notes

# Tasting Notes

_____

_____

_____

_____

_____

_____

_____

_____

_____

_____

_____

_____

_____

_____

# Tasting Notes